Trump Won the True Vote

Polling anomalies, Democratic defections, Independents and late undecided voters

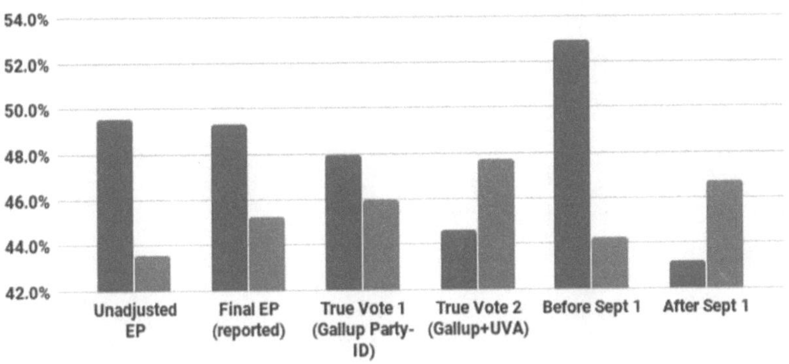

Richard Charnin

Introduction

My goal in writing this book is to present an analysis of the true popular and electoral vote. The True Vote analysis presented in this book indicates that Donald Trump won the popular as well as the electoral vote.

The establishment-dominated media was in the tank for Hillary Clinton in the primary and general elections.

Mainstream media pundits claim that Clinton won the primary and presidential election by nearly three million votes. But they fail to consider the established fact that the recorded vote never equal to the true vote.

The pundits have always assumed that the recorded vote is accurate in every election, but never consider the fraud factor. But historical statistical evidence is conclusive: every election is fraudulent. The recorded vote is never equal to the true vote.

I started following elections in 1952 at the age of nine. My father was an FDR Democrat, a union man. So naturally I became a Democrat and remained one up until the 2016 election. I have posted on elections since 2002 and written three books on election fraud, the most recent on the 2016 primary which was stolen from Bernie Sanders.

The claim that Clinton won the popular vote is quoted ad nauseam in the media, academia and by corrupt politicians. They persist in promoting the fully discredited meme of Russian "hackers" stealing the election from Clinton. But there is not one iota of proof that the Russians had anything to do with it. Included in the appendix are two memos from the Veteran Intelligence Professional for Sanity (VIPS) to Obama and Trump which prove that the Russians did not hack the vote. Election Fraud is always an inside job.

Sanders and Trump drew much larger crowds than Clinton. They won the unscientific online polls by large margins. Trump's Republican base was solid. Clinton's Democratic base was fractured by defecting Sanders voters.

Millions of Sanders primary voters stayed home or voted for Jill Stein or Donald Trump. Trump won Independents by a solid majority (at least 8% higher than Clinton). There was a surge of late deciders to Trump after Labor Day.

Former interim Democratic National Committee chairwoman Donna Brazile delivered a bombshell in her book "Hacked". She claimed that the Hillary Clinton campaign seized control of the Democratic Party as far back as August 2015. Well, this was not a bombshell to researchers who have presented massive evidence that the primary was rigged from Day One.

In **'77 Billion to One: 2016 Election Fraud'**, I provided mathematical evidence that the primary was rigged for Clinton. The exit poll discrepancies were in one direction only; they showed that Sanders did consistently better in the polls than the recorded vote. It was solid proof that the primaries were rigged.

But just because the unadjusted exit polls were quite accurate in prior elections and the 2016 primary does not mean they reflected the true vote in the presidential election.

Six major media corporations (the National Election Pool) fund exit pollster Edison Research. The pollsters had to show that Clinton won the pre-election and unadjusted polls to lend credence to her 2.8 million recorded popular vote margin.

In 2008, 2012 and 2016 my pre-election models exactly forecast the recorded electoral votes. Trump was projected to win 306 recorded electoral votes based on adjustments made to nine final pre-election polls. It also forecast that he would have had 350 electoral votes in a fraud-free election.

Democratic Party-ID was over-weighted in the pre-election and exit polls at the expense of Independents. A post-election exit poll analysis based on the Gallup voter affiliation survey conducted the week prior to the election confirmed the forecast. But Trump did much better than the unadjusted exit polls indicated. The Gallup survey showed that Independents comprised 41% of the electorate on Election Day, with 31% Democrats and 28% Republicans.

An analysis of presidential elections from 1988-2008 indicates that state and national exit poll discrepancies ("red-shift") favored the Republican in every election. The accuracy of the unadjusted exit polls was confirmed by the True Vote Model based on adjustments made to returning voters. The final state and national exit polls were forced to match the recorded vote. But in 2016, several True Vote models could not confirm the unadjusted exit polls or the recorded votes.

In light of the overwhelming media and deep state bias for Clinton, and the proven rigging of the Democratic primary, why should we believe the 2016 pre-election and exit polls?

Exit posters always force state and national unadjusted exit polls to match the recorded vote. This unscientific matching process results in faulty demographic percentages. It also promotes the unstated premise that the final recorded vote was accurate – and there was virtually zero election fraud. This is unacceptable.

The pollsters never provide the location of sampled precincts. How do we know that sampling design was legitimate? To assume that the unadjusted exit polls were accurate just because they were in prior elections is not logical.

Since the final exit polls are always matched to the recorded vote assuming zero fraud, an independent analysis is always necessary. And that is why I wrote this book

Chapter 1: Overview of the Evidence

The MSM interviewed the authors of *Shattered: Inside Hillary Clinton's Doomed Campaign*. I commented on Youtube to Chris Mathews and Brian Williams of MSNBC as well as FOX and CBS on how MSM pollsters rigged the pre-election polls for Clinton.

"Your guests may not have looked at my 2016 Election model. It was based adjustments to final pre-election polls which were biased for Clinton. The Democratic Party-ID share was overstated at the expense of Independents who went solidly for Trump. There is evidence that votes were stolen from Jill Stein – by Clinton".

The primaries were rigged in favor of Clinton. The odds (77 billion to one) were calculated based on exit poll discrepancies. But the 2016 election was different. The corporate media (the National Election Pool) which funds pre-election and exit pollster Edison Research, were heavily biased in favor of Clinton.

Exit poll discrepancies in 1988-2008 proved systemic election fraud. They accurately represented the True Vote – up until the 2016 presidential election. Just because exit polls have proven to be accurate in the past (most recently in the 2016 Democratic primary) does not mean they were accurate in 2016. The fact that Hillary won the popular recorded vote by 2.8 million does not mean she won the True Vote. They are never the same.

The following states flipped to Trump from the unadjusted exit poll to the recorded vote and the Gallup-adjusted exit poll: FL MI NC PA WI (MN flipped to Clinton).

California (3.77), Illinois (0.72) and New York (0.78) provided 5.27 million of Clinton's adjusted margin in the 28 states. Trump won the other 25 states by 3.7 million votes.

So what changed in 2016? The establishment was in the tank for Clinton. Pre-election and exit polls were biased in her favor. Trump won the primaries easily; Clinton had to cheat Bernie.

Trump and Bernie drew big crowds, Clinton drew small crowds. Trump and Bernie won (non-scientific) online debate polls by large margins. In the 2016 Democratic primary: 11 of 26 unadjusted exit polls exceeded the MoE for Sanders.

Exit Poll Democratic Party ID was inflated. **Millions of Sanders voters stayed home or voted for Stein or Trump.** Trump and Sanders each won Independents by 10%. Trump had a higher percentage of Republicans than Clinton had of Democrats.

Clinton's 2.9 million recorded vote margin is bogus. Mainstream media pre-election and exit polls were rigged for Clinton. She won the Recorded Vote 48.3-46.2% but ...

THE RECORDED VOTE IS NEVER EQUAL TO THE TRUE VOTE.

The 2016 Election Model exactly forecast Trump's 306 recorded electoral vote. But he had approximately 351 after adjusting for late undecided voters. The True Vote Model indicates that Trump won by 48-44% (5 million votes). Gallup Party ID was 41I-31D-28R.

Election analysts calculated that Clinton won the electoral vote by 292-246 based on the unadjusted exit polls. Clinton won the unadjusted exit poll and Trump the recorded vote in WI, NC, MI and PA. In MN, Trump won the unadjusted exit poll and Clinton the recorded vote.

But just because the unadjusted exit polls were excellent indicators of fraud in the past does not mean they were correct in 2016. It is highly likely that the unadjusted exit polls were also biased for Clinton. Exit poll discrepancies favored Clinton in the Rust belt and Red states.

The polls matched the recorded vote in large states (i.e. CA). If the recorded vote was bogus, then the unadjusted exit polls must have also overstated Clinton shares. In NY the 5% discrepancy favored Trump.

The exit polls were the basis for recounting MI, WI and PA. But why were there no recounts in states that Trump narrowly won? The unadjusted exit polls look suspicious in states where they closely matched the recorded vote: CA IL MI TX MN WA NY. Clinton's California margin exceeded Obama's by an implausible 6%. An unknown number of illegals were encouraged to vote by Obama.

Unadjusted and reported exit polls were compared to the estimated the True Vote. The TVM was based on the Gallup voter affiliation national survey. The unadjusted polls over-weighted Democratic party-ID and Clinton's share of Independents.

The 2016 Election Model compared 28 unadjusted state exit polls vs. Recorded Vote vs. True Vote. Twenty-three states were not exit-polled so the recorded vote was assumed.

Exit polls and the True Vote Model indicated that the 1968, 1988, 2000 and 2004 elections were stolen. In the 1988-2012 elections, the Democrats won the True Vote and the unadjusted exit polls 52-42%. They won the recorded vote by 48-46%.

In 2012, the exit pollsters stopped asking respondents who they voted for in the prior election. The question was the key to proving fraud in prior elections. For example, in order to match the 2004 recorded vote, the adjusted National Exit Poll indicated that the number of returning Bush 2000 voters was greater than the number still living. So the pollsters decided to no longer ask the question. Just 31 states were exit polled in 2012 and 28 in 2016.

The media giants who fund the pollsters claimed it was too expensive. Trump won all 25 scenarios in a True Vote Sensitivity Analysis based on returning 2012 voters. The pollster's track record is the "tell". Unadjusted exit polls are always forced to match the recorded vote. Only a subset of states are polled. Pollsters never reveal the precincts polled so there is no way of knowing if the sample was truly random. Exit pollsters have never explained the rationale for forcing the unadjusted polls to match the recorded vote.

So why should we believe the 2016 pre-election and exit polls knowing that the media was in the tank for Hillary? In its desperation to explain Clinton's defeat, the corporate controlled media keeps repeating the lie that the Russian hacked the election even though there is not one piece of evidence to support that bogus claim.

Obviously exit polls can be rigged by polling precincts which are not representative of the electorate. There is no way to determine the True Vote unless pre-election and exit polls are analyzed for anomalies

A post-election state exit poll analysis based on Gallup-adjusted national voter affiliation exactly confirmed the forecast model. Trump did much better than the unadjusted exit polls indicated. Just because the polls were accurate in prior elections does not mean they were in 2016.

Rigged voting machines are far more lethal than disenfranchised or illegal voters. The establishment controls the voting machines. The establishment was heavily for Clinton.

Trump won Ohio by 51.7-43.6%. But the unadjusted poll indicates that he won by just 47.1-47.0%. To match the unadjusted poll, Clinton needed to win Independents by an implausible 50-35%. However, the final Ohio exit poll (matched to the recorded vote) indicated that Trump won Independents by 51-38%.

Humboldt County, CA is the only one in the U.S. which has an Open Source vote count/audit system. Sanders had his highest CA share in Humboldt (71%). So did Jill Stein. She had 6% compared to 1% elsewhere.

According to investigative reporter Greg Palast, seven million minority votes were suppressed (one million via Crosscheck), the majority favoring Clinton. Palast claims Clinton won the popular vote. But consider these factors: Illegal voters were estimated at 1-5 million. Obama encouraged illegals to vote. Votes were flipped to Clinton on central tabulators. Clinton benefactor and globalist George Soros had an interest in voting machines in 16 states.

Black and Hispanic voters and college-educated voters leaned toward the Democrats. But Clinton did not get the turnout from these groups that she needed. Black voters did not show up as they did for Barack Obama in 2008 and 2012. One third of the nearly 700 counties that voted for Obama went for Trump

According to the adjusted National Exit Poll (NEP), Clinton defeated Trump among women 54-42%. But Trump won white women 53-43%. Two-thirds of white women without degrees voted for Trump.

White working class men who voted solidly for Trump were joined by their wives, daughters, sisters and mothers. White voters without college degrees were one-third of Obama votes in 2012. They filled the gap between upper-class whites and working-class nonwhites. Trump gained roughly 15% of them compared to Romney in 2012.

Hillary Clinton pandered to Wall Street oligarchs, alienated Russia, and rehabilitated Republican neocons. The campaign violated FEC Super PAC coordination rules and conspired with party officials on everything from political attacks to debate questions. She ignored Wisconsin during the general election.

The NEP indicates that of the 26% of voters who decided after Oct.1; 48% voted for Trump and 40% for Clinton. Clinton led voters who decided before Oct.1 by 51-45%. The NEP also showed that 40% of voters decided after Sept.1. Trump won them by 48-42%. Clinton won voters who decided before Sept.1 by 52.5-45.0%.

The third-party recorded vote is another clue that Clinton's vote was rigged. According to the NEP, 2.5% of voters who decided before Sept.1 voted for a third party candidate; 10% after Oct.1. Jill Stein had just 1% of the recorded vote. Could it be that Jill really had at least 3% of which 2% or more were shifted to Clinton?

Jill Stein asked for recounts in three states Trump barely won. Recounts in MI and WI showed that Trump did better than reported. Wayne County had more votes than registered voters. The Clinton campaign joined in. Jill had just one percent of the vote in each of the three states, which Trump narrowly won. Why did she not request a recount in the states he barely lost?

In Wisconsin nearly 3 million votes **were recounted. Trump picked up 131 votes and won by 22,748 votes. Bev Harris mentioned specific Democrat-controlled cities that were very late in reporting votes. Were they "adjusting" the totals using GEMS software?** Harris mentioned Milwaukee as one of the cities that took forever to report.

During the recount Wisconsin was mostly done, except for **Milwaukee which was coming in slowly. The interim hand-count totals were thousands of votes out of line with the numbers generated by GEMS**. Since Wisconsin had physical ballots, the only way to rig the vote was to slow down the Milwaukee hand recount so it wasn't finished by the deadline. The secretary of state would be forced to use the original GEMS-adjusted numbers and certify that the election had not been tampered with.

In Pennsylvania, a federal judge rejected a Green Party-backed request for a presidential recount in Pennsylvania. Trump beat Clinton by 44,000 votes out of 6 million cast after weeks of counting provisional and overseas ballots.

In Michigan, a federal judge halted the recount. Trump won **Michigan by 11,000 votes out of nearly 4.8 million votes cast.** Hillary Clinton won overwhelmingly in Wayne County with 95% of the vote. Sixty percent of the precincts in Wayne County had to be disqualified from the statewide recount because of "irregularities."

According to Fox News Judge Andrew Napolitano, the irregularities look "organized" and "government involved." County records prepared after the irregularities were discovered revealed that 37% of Detroit precincts registered more votes than voters during the election. **In** Wayne County, there were optical scanners in 248 of the city's 662 precincts. The precincts were among those that couldn't be counted during a statewide presidential recount following a decision by the Michigan Supreme Court.

State records show that 10.6 percent of the precincts in the 22 counties couldn't be recounted because of state law that bars recounts for unbalanced counts or broken seals. In Detroit, officials couldn't recount votes in 392 precincts (60 percent). Two-thirds of the precincts had too many votes. About 20 precincts had ballot boxes opened during the recount with fewer ballots than poll workers had recorded on Election Day.

Chapter 2: The Rigged Democratic Primary

The 2016 Democratic primary finally awakened the public to Election Fraud. Millions of voters who were unaware or in denial came to realize that our election system was rigged and that the mainstream media is complicit in covering up Election Fraud.

The media and its cadre of exit poll naysayers in the corporate media don't dare mention the third-rail of American politics – election fraud. The media pundits remain silent on electronic vote rigging. They maintain that the exit polls are inaccurate and call truth-seeking activists conspiracy buffs.

Overwhelming evidence shows that Sanders won the primaries, despite the 3 million Clinton vote margin repeated endlessly in the media. He won the vast majority of 18-34 year-old voters. His positions on Wall Street corruption, universal health care, eliminating student debt, etc. made him an overwhelming favorite among young voters.

Donna Brazile, the former interim Democratic National Committee chairwoman delivered a bombshell: the Hillary Clinton campaign seized control of the Democratic Party as far back as August 2015.

Brazile said that DNC CEO Amy Dacey signed an agreement with Clinton Campaign Manager Robby Mook in August 2015 known as the Joint Fundraising Agreement between the DNC, Hillary Victory Fund and Hillary for America. It stipulated that the Clinton campaign would raise money to invest in the DNC in return for Clinton controlling the party's finances, strategy and money raised. The DNC was required to consult with the campaign about "staffing, budgeting, data, analytics and mailings".

"Obama left the party $24 million in debt – $15 million in bank debt and more than $8 million owed to vendors after the 2012 campaign and had been paying that off very slowly," Brazile wrote. "Obama's campaign was not scheduled to pay it off until 2016. Hillary for America (the campaign) and the Hillary Victory Fund (its joint fundraising vehicle with the DNC)

had taken care of 80 percent of the remaining debt in 2016, about $10 million, and had placed the party on an allowance."

The Clinton campaign also redirected donations from the Hillary Victory Fund. The individual limit to the fund was maxed out at $353,400 (based on the fact that there were 32 participating states), Brazile said the funds were then directed toward the DNC, which sent the money to the Clinton campaign in Brooklyn. This was possible because individuals can contribute more money to state and national committees than presidential campaigns.

The California primary timeline indicates it was stolen in early voting. Sanders had 43.6% in the California primary on Election Day, June 7. He had 52.7% in ballots counted from June 8-July 7 for a total 46.6% share. View CA counties timeline from June 7 to July 7. But those are the recorded votes. He did much better than 46.6%.

In LA County on Election Day, June 7, Sanders had 33.4% in early voting before 5 pm. He had 42.4% at closing on June 7. He had 45.1% in the final count on July 7. "Election Justice USA asserts that a Capitol Weekly early-voter exit poll conducted across the state of California yielded a 23 percent discrepancy in Los Angeles vote-by-mail ballots compared to the actual results".

In San Diego County on Election Day, Sanders had 35.8% in early voting before 5 pm. He had 44.5% at closing on June 7. He had 48.1% in the final count on July 7. From Ray Lutz: "We won! Press conf details how San Diego County (and many others) cheat on election audits. Court case PROVES election audit fraud in San Diego, where they left out 285,000 ballots from the audit, and then carefully rifled through and pre-counted 192,000 in the audit. Bernie Sanders won 58% to 42% in the polling-place ballots but lost 58% to 42% against HRC in the "rifled through" and precounted vote-by-mail ballots".

Sanders won provisional ballots in a landslide: 62.5- 37.5%. The Later VBMs and Provisionals were not audited at all, and this was the subject of our lawsuit (which we won). The final margin of victory by HRC was 3.75%. The later VBMs and provisional ballots leaves a big hole for undetectable hacking to occur either by a compromised employee or by external hackers with access to the central tabulator, or simply mistakes in tabulating machines.

The margin of victory was only 16,000 votes between Clinton and Sanders in the primary, easily hid in the 285,000 unaudited ballots, and even in those 68,000 accepted but unaudited provisional. Clearly, such blatant violation of the election code is a form of election fraud.

Humboldt County, CA is the only one in the U.S. which uses an Open Source vote counting/audit system. Is it just a coincidence that Bernie Sanders had his highest share in Humboldt (71%)?

On July 25th, 2016, Election Justice USA (EJUSA) released a hundred-page report compiling evidence of massive election fraud during the 2016 Democratic primaries. Election Justice USA is a non-partisan organization that consists of attorneys, technologists, journalists, statisticians, and activists.

Essentially, EJUSA concludes that Bernie Sanders may have lost an upper estimate of 184 pledged delegates due to specific irregularities and instances of fraud. Their conclusions? The combination of voter suppression, registration tampering, voter purging, and the manipulation of computerized voting machines, likely cost Bernie Sanders the election.

Additionally, Election Justice USA found that the computer counts differed widely from the exit poll projections, but only for the Democratic Party primaries. Bernie Sanders' exit poll share exceeded his recorded vote share by greater than the margin of error in 11 of 26 primaries: Alabama, Arizona, Georgia, Massachusetts, New York, Ohio, Mississippi, South Carolina, Texas, Wisconsin, and West Virginia.

Clinton won the average adjusted exit poll (the recorded vote) by 56.6-43.4%. Sanders won the True Vote Model (TVM) by 52.3-47.7%. The only difference between the TVM and the adjusted exit poll is voter turnout.

The TVM uses a combination of the adjusted exit poll vote shares and the latest Gallup Party ID survey percentages as a proxy for voter turnout. But this is conservative; it assumes there was no vote flipping on the central tabulators and/or the DREs. Bernie must have done better than his average 52.3% share.

True Vote Party-ID is estimated for each state based on the proportional change in National Party-ID from 2014 to 2016. The 2-party share of Independents increased from 37.4% to 57.3%.

Sanders may have won as many as 37 primaries and caucuses. The True Vote Model assumes that the Gallup survey of voter preference reflects actual turnout. This was not the case in closed primaries. On the other hand, mostly Bernie voters were purged from the rolls. And the model assumes no vote flipping which is unrealistic.

The model indicates that Bernie won a) 17 of 27 exit polled primaries (including the NV and IA entrance polled caucuses), b) 8 of 12 primaries where there were no exit polls (CA KY MT NM SD DE RI OR) and c) all 12 caucuses with a 65% average share.

Bernie won the recorded vote in 14 caucuses with a 65% share. The model indicates that he won the IA entrance poll with 63.6% and NV with 61.7%.

Just ONE county in the U.S. uses an Open Source System to count votes - Humboldt County, CA. Could that be why Bernie had 71% of the 2-party vote? It was his highest vote share in ALL 58 counties! The system is a deterrent to fraud.

The Humboldt Open Source (TEVS) tabulation system was pioneered in 2006 by Mitch Trachtenberg, a computer programmer, together with Carolyn Crnich, registrar of Humboldt County and Kevin Collins, election integrity activist. The election showed significant problems in the Diebold system they were using in counting votes. TEVS is a vote audit/counting system to double-check the Hart InterCivic system which has performed well, unlike the Diebold system.

The base case estimate is that Sanders had 52% of the total vote in primaries and caucuses. Sanders' exit poll share exceeded his recorded share in 24 of 26 primaries. The probability is 1 in 190,000. The margin of error was exceeded in 11 primaries. The probability is 1 in 77 billion. Was the exit poll shift to Clinton just pure luck? Or is something else going on?

The National Election Pool of six media giants funds exit pollster Edison Research. The published results are always forced to match the recorded vote, assuming zero election fraud. Historically, unadjusted state and national exit polls have favored the Democrat but there is a consistent RED shift to the Republican in the recorded vote. The True Vote Model indicates that the 1988-2008 unadjusted exit polls were accurate.

According to the NY Times, only 9.3% (31 million) of the population (13.6% of eligible adults) were responsible for the nomination of Hillary Clinton and Donald Trump. The Green Papers estimated voter turnout in the Democratic Primaries at 30.5 million votes. Clinton had 55.20%, Sanders 43.14%, and Other 1.66%. For the Republican Primaries, voter turnout was 31.2 million votes with Trump at 44.96%.

The True Vote Model indicates that Sanders won the Democratic Primaries with 52% of the vote. Gallup had partisan identification at near historic lows: Democrats 29%, Republicans 26% and Independents 42%. The margin of error was 3%.

Chapter 3: Biased Pre-election Polls

Trump led 77-22% in **online debate polls** of 4 million respondents. He had 59% in the polls after the first debate.

Clinton won the **CNN "scientific" poll** of 537 respondents by 57-34%. But the poll indicated Trump did better than expected (Better 63%; Worse 21%), confirming Trump's 18% gain in the **online polls** from the first debate.

A New York Times article in 10/14/15 reported that "Hillary Rodham Clinton was the clear victor, according to the opinion shapers in the political world (even conservative commentators)." The Times quoted National Journal columnist Ron Fournier ("Hillary Clinton won"), Slate writer Fred Kaplan ("She crushed it"), New Yorker staffer Ryan Lizza ("Hillary Clinton won because all of her opponents are terrible"), Pollster John Zogby ("Mrs. Clinton was just commanding tonight") Conservative radio host Erick Erickson ("I'm still amazed the other four candidates made Hillary Clinton come off as the likable, reasonable, responsible Democrat").

But a **CNN focus group** participant reported: "*After the debate, they asked all of us in the focus group if we were decided on a candidate. Out of 28 panel members, 5 said they were decided on Clinton, 2 said they were decided on Trump, and 12 said they were going to vote 3rd party. But once they saw the response, they reshot the segment and replaced "3rd party" with "still undecided".*

The **Frank Luntz focus group** came up with an interesting result to the question: *Who are you willing to vote for?*

Four Clinton voters and five undecideds switched to Trump. Before the debate Hillary: 8: Trump: 9. After: Hillary: 4; Trump: 18

Who Won the October 13 Democratic Debate?
Selected Web Polls

Outlet	Sanders %	Clinton %	Respondents
Slate	71	16	--
Time	56	11	235,000
Drudge Report	54	9	315,000
Daily Kos	56	38	22,000
KTWB-TV	78	15	45,000
MSNBC	69	12	18,000
The Street	80	15	13,000

The latest **NBC/WSJ Poll of 447 likely voters** showed Clinton surging to an 11 point lead. But just like the other mainstream media pre-election polls, Independent Party ID percentages conflicted with the **Gallup Party Affiliation Survey**. Was there an **NBC conflict of interest?**

Hillary Clinton courted Republicans and moved to the right while ignoring progressives. Donald Trump courted Democrats who cannot support Clinton. While 45% of Republicans voted for Trump in the Primaries, pre-election polls indicated that very few defected. A small number voted for Hillary Clinton, more for Libertarian candidate Gary Johnson. It is estimated that 10-20% of disaffected Sanders voters did not vote for Clinton.

Bernie or Bust voters promoted a Jill or Bust pledge since Sanders did not run a write-in campaign. How many Bernie or Bust voters have pledged themselves to Jill Stein of the Green Party is unclear, but many donated to Stein. An unscientific Internet poll of 253K respondents conducted by NJ.com had Clinton at 11.4%, Trump at 13.7%, Stein 68.0%, and Johnson 3.0%.

In the Aug. 24 IPSOS/REUTERS poll Clinton had 39%; Trump 36%; Johnson 7%; Stein 3%. The sample of 1,516 Americans included 635

Democrats (41.9%), 527 Republicans (34.8%), 174 Independents (11.5%) and 180 (11.8%) who did not indicate a preference.

The Gallup Party-ID survey indicated 28% Democrats, 28% Republicans and 42% Independents.

In the July 17 IPSOS poll, Independents comprised just 14% of the sample. Stein had 1%. Clinton and Trump were tied. The Reuters/Ipsos poll indicated a Party-ID split of 36% Democrats and 25% Republicans – an apparent contradiction to the polling sample. Assuming the other 39% were Independents, it is a close match to the Gallup Survey.

Sanders won approximately 65% of Independents and 35% of Democrats in the primaries. One would logically expect that Stein would do nearly as well as Sanders against Clinton in a four-way race. They are in essential agreement on major issues – and Clinton has very low approval ratings. But Stein had an implausibly low 3% on Aug. 24 and 1% on July 17.

It was no contest. Sanders beat Clinton by 5-1 according to at least 648,000 viewers. But since when does the public decide who won? The media decides who will run. The fix is always in. Sanders could have had 99% and it would not make a difference.

Oct. 19: 15 Battleground States - Real Clear Politics

Pct	Clinton	Trump	Johnson	Stein
38.7%	40%	48%	8%	4%
31.6%	89%	5%	2%	4%
29.7%	5%	90%	4%	1%
Calc	**45.1%**	**46.9%**	**4.9%**	**3.1%**
Poll	**45.4%**	**42.9%**	**5.4%**	**1.3%**
Diff	**-0.3%**	**4.0%**	**-0.5%**	**1.8%**
15 BG	**45.4%**	**42.9%**	**5.4%**	**1.3%**

	Clinton	Trump	Johnson	Stein	Trump EV	Clinton
AZ	42	44	9	1	11	
CO	45	37	10	3		9
FL	48	44	4	1		29
GA	42	48	4	0	16	
IA	39	43	6	2	6	
ME	44	36	9	3		4
MI	47	37	7	4		16
MN	43	43	4	2		
MO	42	47	4	1	10	
NC	48	47	4	0		15
NV	47	40	7	0		6
OH	45	45	6	1		
PA	47	41	6	1		20
VA	46	43	6	0		13
WI	47	39	1	3		10
WtdAvg	**45.4**	**42.9**	**5.4**	**1.3**	**43**	**122**

Oct. 23: Five Pre-election polls

The Party-ID demographic in five national polls (see **realclearpolitics.com**) varied greatly. Average Party-ID was 40.8D- 33.6R- 25.6 I. Trump leads the Independents in each poll by an average of 40-28%. Theoretically, the polls should have had nearly identical Party-ID weightings.

A **summary analysis** compares the shares to those obtained using the **Gallup party affiliation survey** (40% Independents, 32% Democrats, 28% Republicans).

Clinton led the average of five pre-election polls by 43.0-40.7% with a 302-236 electoral vote. But using the Gallup survey weights, Trump led 41.8-39.3% and 329-209 EV. The IBD/TIPP poll was the only one in which Independents were the largest group (38%) and closely approximated the Gallup affiliation survey.

On Oct. 30, eight pre-election polls showed Trump surging.

Clinton led the 8-poll average 45.4-42.5% with 309 EV. But when Party-ID was replaced by the Gallup survey and 75% of undecided voters were allocated to Trump, he led by 48.2-44.1% with 336 EV.

He had a 92% popular vote win probability. Undecided voters typically break 75% for the challenger. Trump was assumed as the challenger and Clinton the incumbent.

8-Poll.................................. Electoral Vote..... Trump Popular Vote

Average..... Clinton Trump..... Clinton.. Trump...Win Prob (3% MoE).

Poll............ 45.4%... 42.5%....... 309... 229........14%

Adjusted..... 42.8%... 44.2%........ 225.... 313........70%

Undec.........44.1%... 48.2%.........202... 336........92%

% Ind .... 32.5%... 45.1%

Party ID... Ind.... Dem.... Rep

Avg Poll... 27.5% 39.0% 31.9%

Gallup..... 40.0% 32.0% 28.0% (adjusted)

Chapter 4: Election Model Forecast

The model shows that the pre-election polls overstated Clinton's vote by inflating the number of democrats compared to independents and republicans

Recorded Vote: Clinton 48.3-46.2%, Trump 306-232 EV
Recorded Vote Forecast: Trump 44.4-42.9% with 306-232 EV
True Vote Model: Trump 48.5-44.3% with 351-187 EV

Unlike corporate mainstream polls, the 2016 Election Model provided two forecasts: the Recorded and True Vote. Pollsters are usually quite accurate in their projections of the Recorded Vote. But they avoid the fraud factor. **The recorded vote is never equal to the True Vote. Clinton won the recorded vote by 48.3-46.2%.**

The **2016 Election Model** is based on the effects of changes in party affiliation (Dem, Rep, Ind) from 2012 to 2016. **Clinton led the final 9-poll average 45.8-43.3% (298-240 EV).**

In the Election Model forecast, state party-ID weights were adjusted to the Gallup party-affiliation survey weights. Gallup was the only poll dedicated to tracking national party affiliation.

After adjusting the polls to the Gallup survey (40I-32D-28R), undecided voters were allocated (UVA) to derive the final TRUE poll share. Typically the challenger wins the majority (75%) of the undecided vote.

Recorded Vote: Trump wins 44.4-42.9% with 306-232 EV.
True Vote: 75% of undecided voters to Trump.
Trump wins 48.4-44.3% with 352-186 EV.

Forecast Methodology

The 2016 party-ID for each state is calculated by applying a proportional change from the 2012 party-ID based on the Gallup 2016 national survey. The popular vote win probability and corresponding Electoral Vote are estimated for each pre-election poll. State votes are forecast by applying national poll shares to the state party-ID.

The electoral vote is calculated two ways:
1) Snapshot EV: sum of candidate's state electoral votes and
2) Expected EV: state win probability times the electoral vote

Sensitivity Analysis tables show the effect of incremental vote shares on the total vote. Assuming 75% UVA to Trump, there was a 96% probability that he would win the popular vote.

UVA	Trump	Clinton	EV	WinProb
50%	47.1	45.6	310	75%
60%	47.6	45.1	332	86%
75%	48.5	44.3	352	96%

Party-ID

	Ind	Dem	Rep
Gallup: Nov1-6	36%	31%	27%
Gallup: Nov 9-13	40%	30%	27%
Gallup: Election Day	41%	31%	28%
National Exit Poll	31%	36%	33%
9 Pre-election Polls	29.6%	38.7%	30.2%

Party-ID 9 Polls

Gallup	Pct	Clinton	Trump	Johnson	Stein
Independent	40.0%	33.8%	43.6%	8.9%	3.8%
Democrat	32.0%	88.1%	6.9%	1.3%	1.7%
Republican	28.0%	5.6%	87.8%	3.9%	0.3%
Pre UVA	94.7%	43.3%	44.2%	5.1%	2.1%
Votes	128,963	55,792	57,007	6,540	2,757
Electoral Vote	538	232	306		
UVA	100.0%	44.5%	48.2%	5.1%	2.1%
Votes	136,216	60,641	65,720	6,908	2,912
Evote	538	187	351		
Recorded	98.77%	48.25%	46.17%	3.29%	1.07%
Votes	136,216	65,719	62,890	4,483	1,454
EVote		232	306		

Pre-election Polls	Ind	Party-ID		Poll		Elect Vote		75%	UVA Trump	
		Dem	Rep	HRC	DJT	HRC	DJT	Und	HRC	DJT
Reuters	17%	45%	32%	42.0%	39.0%	298	240	10%	44.5%	46.5%
IBD	37%	34%	29%	43.0%	45.0%	202	336	2.0%	43.5%	46.5%
Rasmussen	32%	40%	27%	45.0%	43.0%	313	225	6.0%	46.5%	47.5%
Quinnipiac	26%	40%	34%	47.0%	40.0%	378	160	5.0%	48.3%	43.8%
Fox News	25%	43%	29%	48.0%	44.0%	317	221	1.0%	48.3%	44.8%
CNN	43%	31%	26%	49.0%	44.0%	362	176	2.0%	49.5%	45.5%
ABC	29%	37%	30%	47.0%	44.0%	317	221	3.0%	47.8%	46.3%
Gravis	27%	40%	33%	47.0%	45.0%	294	244	4.0%	48.0%	48.0%
LA Times	30%	38%	32%	44.0%	47.0%	202	336	0.0%	44.0%	47.0%
Average	29.6%	38.7%	30.2%	45.8%	43.4%	298	240	5.4%	46.7%	46.2%

ADJUST	Ind			Poll Gallup		EV pre UVA		75%	UVA Gallup	
	HRC	DJT	Diff	HRC	DJT	HRC	DJT	Und	HRC	DJT
Reuters	21%	33%	12%	36.0%	36.8%	239	299	14.%	39.5%	47.4%
IBD	30%	47%	17%	41.9%	45.3%	202	336	2.0%	42.4%	46.9%
Rasmussen	30%	42%	12%	40.6%	45.3%	167	371	7.0%	42.4%	50.6%
Quinnipiac	37%	42%	5%	44.7%	40.8%	335	203	5.9%	46.2%	45.2%
Fox News	39%	44%	5%	45.8%	43.9%	298	240	1.4%	46.1%	44.9%
CNN	43%	44%	1%	48.6%	44.4%	335	203	2.0%	49.2%	46.0%
ABC	40%	49%	9%	46.8%	47.0%	249	289	0.6%	46.9%	47.5%
Gravis	32%	43%	11%	43.6%	45.5%	216	322	8.0%	45.6%	51.5%
LA Times	32%	52%	20%	41.7%	48.2%	85	453	2.0%	42.2%	49.7%
Average	33.8%	44.0%	10.2%	43.3%	44.1%	236	302	4.8%	44.5%	47.7%

Reuters	Pct	Clinton	Trump	Johnson	Stein	Other
Ind	17%	21%	33%	15%	8%	23.0%
Dem	45%	81%	10%	4%	3%	2.0%
Rep	32%	6%	90%	2%	1%	1.0%
Calc	88.9%	41.9%	38.9%	5.0%	3.0%	11.1%
Poll	90.0%	42.0%	39.0%	6.0%	3.0%	10.0%
Gallup	85.9%	36.0%	36.8%	8.7%	4.4%	14.1%

IBD/TIPP	Pct	Clinton	Trump	Johnson	Stein	Other
Ind	37%	30%	47%	16%	3%	4.0%
Dem	34%	87%	7%	0%	3%	3.0%
Rep	29%	6%	85%	5%	0%	4.0%
Calc	96.3%	42.4%	44.4%	7.4%	2.1%	3.7%
Poll	98.0%	43.0%	45%	8.0%	2.0%	2.0%
Gallup	98.0%	41.9%	45.3%	8.5%	2.2%	2.0%

Rasmussen	Pct	Clinton	Trump	Johnson	Stein	Other
Ind	32%	30%	42%	6%	4%	18.0%
Dem	40%	85%	12%	1%	1%	1.0%
Rep	27%	5%	88%	5%	1%	1.0%
Calc	92.6%	45.0%	42.0%	3.7%	2.0%	7.4%
Poll	94.0%	45.0%	43.0%	4.0%	2.0%	6.0%
Gallup	93.0%	40.6%	45.3%	4.8%	2.3%	7.0%

Quinnipac	Pct	Clinton	Trump	Johnson	Stein	Other
Ind	26%	37%	42%	8%	2%	11.0%
Dem	40%	90%	4%	3%	1%	2.0%
Rep	34%	4%	81%	11%	1%	3.0%
Calc	95.3%	47.0%	40.1%	7.0%	1.3%	4.7%
Poll	95.0%	47.0%	40.0%	7.0%	1.0%	5.0%
Gallup	94.1%	44.7%	40.8%	7.2%	1.4%	5.9%

Fox News	Pct	Clinton	Trump	Johnson	Stein	Other
Ind	25%	39%	44%	11%	4%	2.0%
Dem	43%	89%	7%	2%	2%	0.0%
Rep	29%	6%	87%	5%	1%	1.0%
Calc	96.2%	49.8%	39.2%	5.1%	2.2%	3.8%
Poll	99.0%	48.0%	44.0%	5.0%	2.0%	1.0%
Gallup	98.6%	45.8%	43.9%	6.4%	2.5%	1.4%

CNN	Pct	Clinton	Trump	Johnson	Stein	Other
Ind	43%	43%	44%	6%	4%	3.0%
Dem	31%	93%	6%	0%	1%	0.0%
Rep	26%	6%	89%	2%	0%	3.0%
Calc	97.9%	48.9%	43.9%	3.1%	2.0%	2.1%
Poll	98.0%	49.0%	44.0%	3.0%	2.0%	2.0%
Gallup	98.0%	48.6%	44.4%	3.0%	1.9%	2.0%

ABC	Pct	Clinton	Trump	Johnson	Stein	Other
Ind	29%	40%	49%	7%	4%	0.0%
Dem	37%	90%	7%	0%	2%	1.0%
Rep	30%	7%	90%	2%	0%	1.0%
Calc	95.3%	47.0%	43.8%	2.6%	1.9%	4.7%
Poll	97.0%	47.0%	44.0%	4.0%	2.0%	3.0%
Gallup	99.4%	46.8%	47.0%	3.4%	2.2%	0.6%

Gravis	Pct	Clinton	Trump	Johnson	Stein	Other
Ind	27%	32%	43%	3%	2%	20.0%
Dem	40%	92%	7%	0%	1%	0.0%
Rep	33%	5%	93%	2%	0%	0.0%
Calc	94.6%	47.1%	45.1%	1.5%	0.9%	5.4%
Poll	96%	47.0%	45.0%	3.0%	1.0%	4.0%
Gallup	92%	43.6%	45.5%	1.8%	1.1%	8.0%

LA Times	Pct	Clinton	Trump	Johnson	Stein	Other
Ind	30%	32%	52%	10%	5%	1.0%
Dem	38%	86%	10%	2%	1%	1.0%
Rep	30%	6%	92%	4%	0%	-2.0%
Calc	97.9%	44.1%	47.0%	5.0%	1.9%	2.1%
Poll	100.0%	44.0%	47.0%	7.0%	2.0%	0.0%
Gallup	98.0%	41.7%	48.2%	5.8%	2.3%	2.0%

The Battleground

In 16 battleground states, Trump won the recorded vote by 48.0-45.9%. Clinton led the pre-election polls by 44.5-44.1%, a 2.5% discrepancy between the polls and corresponding recorded votes. Clinton won the 16 unadjusted exit polls by 47.4-45.6%.

Allocating undecided voters (UVA), Trump leads the 16-poll average by 46.6-45.3%. The Gallup National Voter affiliation survey (40Ind-32Dem-28Rep) was the basis used to derive each state's Party-ID. Trump leads by 48.9-43.1% with these adjustments.

Polling summary: 16 Battleground states

Unweighted average:
Trump won the recorded vote by 48.0-45.9%.
Clinton won the pre-election polls by 44.5-44.1%.
Trump won the UVA-adjusted polls by 46.6-45.3%.
Trump won the Gallup Party-ID adjusted polls by 48.9-43.1%.
Clinton won the unadjusted exit polls by 47.4-45.6%

Weighted average (56.8 million votes):
Trump won the recorded vote by 48.4-46.1%.
Clinton won the pre-election polls by 45.0-44.7%.
Trump won the UVA-adjusted polls by 47.0-45.7%.
Trump won the Gallup Party-ID adjusted polls by 48.5-43.9%.
Clinton won the unadjusted exit polls by 47.5-46.1%

	Poll			Recorded		Chg		Final			Unadj		
	DJT	HRC	Marg	DJT	HRC	Marg	Marg	DJT	HRC	Marg	HRC	DJT	
Avg	44.1	44.5	-0.41	48.0	45.9	2.1	2.5	46.6	45.3	1.37	45.6	47.4	-1.8
Wtd	44.7	45.0	-0.28	48.4	46.1	2.3	2.6	47.0	45.7	1.34	46.1	47.5	-1.4
AZ	46.3	42.3	4.0	48.1	44.6	3.5	-0.5	48.3	43.0	5.4	46.9	43.6	3.3
CO	40.4	43.3	-2.9	43.3	48.2	-4.9	-2.0	44.3	44.6	-0.3	41.5	46.5	-5.0
FL	46.6	46.4	0.2	48.6	47.4	1.2	1.0	48.1	46.9	1.2	46.4	47.7	-1.3
GA	49.2	44.4	4.8	50.5	45.4	5.1	0.3	50.0	44.7	5.4	48.2	46.8	1.4
IA	44.3	41.3	3.0	51.2	41.7	9.5	6.5	47.6	42.4	5.2	48.0	44.1	3.9
ME	39.5	44.0	-4.5	44.9	47.8	-2.9	1.6	44.5	45.7	-1.2	40.2	51.2	-11
MI	42.0	45.4	-3.4	47.3	47.0	0.3	3.7	45.4	46.5	-1.2	46.8	46.8	0
MN	39.0	49.0	-10.0	44.9	46.4	-1.5	8.5	40.8	48.6	-7.8	45.8	45.7	0.1
MO	50.3	39.3	11.0	56.4	37.9	18.5	7.5	52.0	39.9	12.2	51.2	42.8	8.4
NV	45.8	45.0	0.8	45.5	47.9	-2.4	-3.2	47.2	45.5	1.8	42.8	48.7	-5.9
NH	42.7	43.3	-0.6	46.5	46.8	-0.3	0.3	45.9	44.4	1.6	44.2	49.4	-5.2
NC	46.5	45.5	1.0	49.9	46.2	3.7	2.7	49.2	46.4	2.8	46.5	48.6	-2.1
OH	45.8	42.3	3.5	51.3	43.2	8.1	4.6	48.3	43.1	5.2	47.1	47.0	0.1
PA	44.3	46.2	-1.9	48.2	47.5	0.7	2.6	47.2	47.2	0.0	46.1	50.5	-4.4
VA	42.3	47.3	-5.0	44.4	49.8	-5.4	-0.4	44.6	48.1	-3.5	43.2	50.9	-7.7
WI	40.3	46.8	-6.5	47.2	46.5	0.7	7.2	42.9	47.7	-4.8	44.3	48.2	-3.9

Adjusted Pre-election polls

This analysis shows that although Clinton won the Recorded Vote by 48.3-46.2% (2.8 million votes), Trump won the True Vote.

Plausible adjustments made to nine pre-election polls in the True Vote Model are the core of the analysis: Reuters, IBD, Rasmussen, Quinnipiac, Fox News, CNN, ABC, Gravis, LA Times. The polls had Clinton winning by 45.8-43.6% with 298-240 electoral votes.

Adjusting Party-ID to the Gallup voter affiliation survey, Trump won by the polls by 43.4-43.1% with 306-232 electoral votes. After allocating 75% of undecided voters to Trump (the de-facto challenger) the True Vote Model indicates that he won by 48.2-44.5% (5.1 million votes) with 336 electoral votes. His expected EV was 351. Historically, in elections where the incumbent was unpopular, challengers won 65-85% of undecided voters. Clinton was the unpopular de-facto incumbent, especially after she stole the primary from Bernie Sanders.

Model Results

Pre-election poll averages based on:
Party-ID: Clinton 45.8-43.6
Gallup voter affiliation: Trump 43.4-43.1
Forecast Model (post-UVA)

Party-ID (9 Pre-election poll average): Clinton 46.7-46.2
Gallup Party-ID: Trump 48.2-44.5
Trump Electoral votes: Pre and post UVA

Snapshot EV: pre-UVA: 306 (exact forecast); post-UVA: 336
Expected EV: Pre UVA: 289; post UVA: 351

Method

Calculate the average of 9 final pre-election polls based on Party-ID and average vote shares to the Gallup national voter affiliation survey.

9-poll average Party-ID: 28.9I-38.7D-31.9R
Gallup voter affiliation survey: 40I-32D-28R

Gallup Voter Affiliation

1- Nov. 1-6: 36I, 31D, 27R (6 other)
2- Nov. 9-13: 40I, 30D, 27R (3 other)
Average (Election Day) : 38I, 30.5D, 27R (4.5 other)

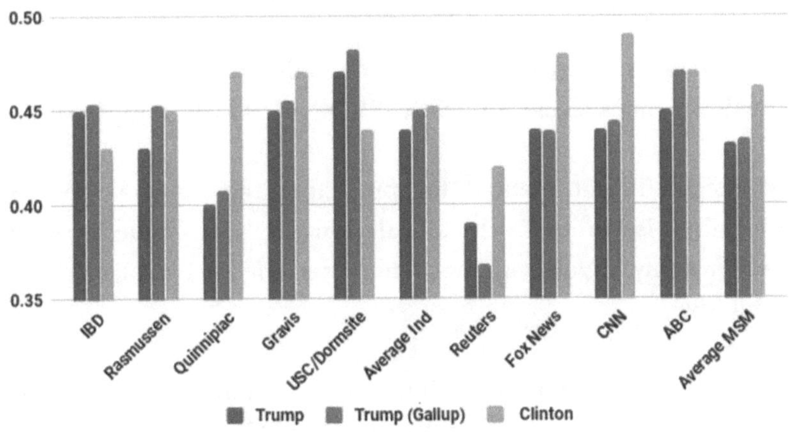

Trump Pre-election Polls with Gallup Voter Affilation

Forecasting the Electoral Vote

Regardless of the forecast method used, only state win probabilities are needed to calculate the EXPECTED ELECTORAL VOTE. A simulation is required to calculate the electoral vote WIN PROBABILITY.

$$EV = \sum P(i) * EV(i), \text{ for } i = 1, 51$$

Calculating the expected electoral vote is a three-step process:
1. Project the 2-party vote share V(i) for each state(i) as the sum of the final pre-election poll share PS(i) and undecided voter allocation UVA (i): V(i)= PS(i) + UVA(i)

2. Compute the probability of winning each state given the projected share and the margin of error (95% confidence level): P (i) = NORMDIST (V (i), 0.5, MoE/1.96, true)

3. Compute the expected electoral vote as the sum of each state's win probability times its electoral vote: $EV = \sum P(i) * EV(i)$ for i = 1,51

The most efficient method for projecting the electoral vote win probability is **Monte Carlo simulation.** This technique is widely used in many diverse applications when an analytical solution is prohibitive.

The 2012 Presidential True Vote and Election Fraud Simulation **Model snapshot forecast exactly matched Obama's 332 Electoral Votes. The model also forecast a 320.7 theoretical (expected) EV and a 320 simulation (mean) EV.**

In the 2008 Election Model, **Obama's 365.3 expected theoretical electoral vote was a near-perfect match to his 365 recorded EV. The** 5000 trial Monte Carlo 365.8 simulation EV converged to the theoretical 365.3 expected EV. Obama's projected 53.1% share was a close match to the 52.9% recorded vote. He had a 100% win probability. But the likely voter (LV) polls understated Obama's true vote.

National Registered Voter (RV) polls projected that Obama would win a 57% share. This was confirmed by 1) the True Vote Model (58%, 420 EV), 2) the unadjusted state exit poll aggregate (58%, 420 EV) and 3) the unadjusted National Exit Poll (61%).

The 2016 party-ID for each state was calculated based on the proportional change from 2012 party-ID to the 2016 Gallup survey.
2012: 40.3% Dem, 35.4% Rep, 24.7% Independent
2016: 32.0% Dem, 28.0% Rep, 40.0% Independent

Sensitivity Analysis
15 scenarios (pre-UVA) based on Trump's share of Rep and Ind
Best Case: Trump 45.0-42.7%
Base Case: Trump 43.4-43.1%
Worst Case: Clinton 43.5-41.9%

Electoral Vote Scenarios
Recorded EV = 306
Forecast EV (pre-UVA) = 306

Expected Electoral Vote
P (i) = probability of winning the state, EV (i) electoral vote.
Margin of Error (MoE) = 2.5%
Expected EV = $\sum$ P (i) * EV (i), for i = 1, 51

Pre-UVA: Expected EV = 305.5

Post-UVA: Expected EV = 351
Undecided voter allocation (UVA): 75% to Trump

	EV	Clinton	Trump	HRC	DJT	Win Prob
AK	3	33.3%	49.2%		3	100.0%
AL	9	37.8%	50.7%		9	100.0%
AR	6	39.8%	48.3%		6	100.0%
AZ	11	38.5%	47.3%		11	100.0%
CA	55	46.0%	40.9%	55		1.0%
CO	9	39.6%	46.2%		9	99.9%
CT	7	44.7%	40.3%	7		2.2%
DC	3	65.8%	23.9%	3		0.0%
DE	3	47.9%	39.7%	3		0.0%
FL	29	42.6%	44.6%		29	82.4%
GA	16	40.9%	47.4%		16	99.8%
HI	4	46.9%	41.7%	4		1.0%
IA	6	39.9%	45.8%		6	99.6%
ID	4	33.7%	54.0%		4	100.0%
IL	20	46.1%	42.3%	20		4.5%
IN	11	39.8%	48.3%		11	100.0%
KS	6	34.5%	51.9%		6	100.0%
KY	8	39.9%	45.4%		8	99.4%
LA	8	39.2%	45.5%		8	99.8%
MA	11	46.5%	37.2%	11		0.0%
MD	10	51.6%	36.7%	10		0.0%
ME	4	41.4%	43.9%		4	87.3%
MI	16	44.3%	43.8%	16		41.0%
MN	10	43.9%	44.5%		10	61.1%
MO	10	40.6%	47.7%		10	99.9%

	HRC	DJT	HRC	DJT	Prob
MS	39.8%	48.7%		6	100.0%
MT	36.5%	51.9%		3	100.0%
NC	44.8%	42.2%	15		11.5%
ND	38.7%	49.7%		3	100.0%
NE	36.2%	51.6%	1	4	100.0%
NH	38.7%	46.3%		4	100.0%
NJ	43.4%	41.0%	14		13.6%
NM	46.8%	41.0%	5		0.5%
NV	43.0%	44.2%		6	70.4%
NY	49.6%	37.7%	29		0.0%
OH	41.9%	46.5%		18	97.8%
OK	42.7%	46.2%		7	93.9%
OR	45.4%	42.7%	7		11.5%
PA	46.8%	42.1%	20		2.0%
RI	49.1%	35.4%	4		0.0%
SC	40.6%	47.7%		9	99.9%
SD	37.9%	50.0%		3	100.0%
TN	38.2%	50.0%		11	100.0%
TX	40.4%	47.3%		38	99.9%
UT	28.0%	45.5%		6	100.0%
VA	41.5%	46.7%		13	99.0%
VT	47.0%	40.9%	3		0.3%
WA	43.0%	46.4%		12	93.1%
WI	43.0%	45.5%		10	86.7%
WV	48.5%	39.4%	5		0.0%

Gallup 2016 Voter Affiliation

2016	Repub %	Indep %	Dem %	Other %	Repub %	Indep + other %	Dem %
Average	**27.7**	**39.5**	**30.4**	**2.3**	**27.7**	**41.9**	**30.4**
Dec 7-11	28	39	29	4	28	43	29
Nov 9-13	**27**	**40**	**30**	**3**	**27**	**43**	**30**
Oct 5-9	27	36	32	5	27	41	32
Sep 14-18	27	40	32	1	27	41	32
Sep 7-11	29	38	31	2	29	40	31
Aug 3-7	27	38	31	4	27	42	31
Jul 13-17	28	42	28	2	28	44	28
Jun 14-23	28	39	31	2	28	41	31
Jun 1-5	27	41	30	2	27	43	30
May 18-22	27	45	28	0	27	45	28
May 4-8	31	37	30	2	31	39	30
Apr 6-10	25	44	31	0	25	44	31
Mar 2-6	26	38	32	4	26	42	32
Feb 3-7	30	37	30	3	30	40	30
Jan 21-25	29	39	31	1	29	40	31

Chapter 5: Biased Exit Polls

Unadjusted exit polls are always forced to match the recorded vote. The false premise assumes ZERO fraud in every election.

In the 1988-2008 presidential elections. Democrats led the unadjusted exit polls by 52-42%, but won the recorded vote by just 48-46%. The pattern was unmistakable. There was a systemic red-shift in the exit polls. The probability of the discrepancy was 1 in trillions. I confirmed the polls with the True Vote Model based on returning voters. Elections were stolen from Gore in 2000 and Kerry in 2004 – and probably from Dukakis in 1988.

In 2016, Clinton led the average of nine pre-election national polls 45.8-43.3%. Trump led Independents by 10% (43.6-33.8%), but by just 4% (46-42%) in the final National Exit Poll (matched to the recorded vote).

In 2016, the media was in the tank for Clinton. The unadjusted exit polls proved the primaries were rigged for Hillary. In the primaries, there was a major exit poll red-shift from Sanders to Clinton in the vote. Eleven of 26 exit polls exceeded the margin of error – a 1 in 77 billion probability.

The six media corporations who fund pollster Edison Research would be embarrassed if Trump won the exit polls, the true popular vote and the electoral. They had to remove any doubt that Clinton won the popular vote as predicted by the pre-election polls. So Clinton won the exit polls along with the popular recorded vote in key battleground states. There could be no repeat of the Democratic primary exit poll anomalies.

It is standard operating procedure for the exit pollsters to force state and national unadjusted exit polls to match the recorded vote, why should they be trusted in the 2016 election? Especially since a) they were in the tank for Clinton and 2) never provide the location of precincts polled and actual respondent data. To assume that the unadjusted exit polls were pristine in 2016 just because they were fairly accurate in prior elections is not logical.

The pollsters force the exit polls to match the recorded vote count data, so one cannot claim that the exit polls are not subject to manipulation -or that the votes were not rigged. True Vote models confirmed the exit polls – until the 2016 presidential election. In 2012 just 31 states were exit polled; in 2016, just 28 were.

The National Election Pool (NEP) funds the pollsters. The NEP claimed that it was too expensive to poll every state, so they left out states that were non-competitive. That made it difficult to forecast the True Vote.

The ballots are not available for public inspection. We are denied access to evidence that would allow a determination of whether the election has been manipulated. The trend has been for ballots to be removed from public record status so that they are no longer available for public information requests.

One positive aspect of the 2016 election is widespread recognition that election fraud is a reality. But the political establishment and mainstream media spreads the fiction that the Russians hacked the election.

According to exit polls conducted by Edison Research, Clinton won four key battleground states (NC, PA, WI, and FL) in the 2016 Presidential Election that she lost.

Trump won the OH reported vote by 51.7-43.6%. But according to the CNN- unadjusted exit poll, he won by just 47.1-47.0%. Does the discrepancy indicate that votes were rigged for Trump?

The unadjusted exit poll discrepancy is explained by the implausible difference between Trump and Clinton's share of Independents.

In order to match the unadjusted Ohio exit poll, assuming the recorded exit poll Party-ID and vote shares. Clinton needed to win Independents by 50-35%.

Some election integrity analysts claim that it is wrong to assume that the unadjusted exit poll party-ID is identical to the adjusted (recorded) party-ID. But if they differ, then the unadjusted exit poll vote shares would need to be different from the adjusted final exit poll shares.

Both pre-election and post-election analysis indicates that the exit polls and recorded vote counts were wrong. The media and the establishment slammed Trump and extolled Clinton even though she was in danger of being indicted for destruction of incriminating e-mails.

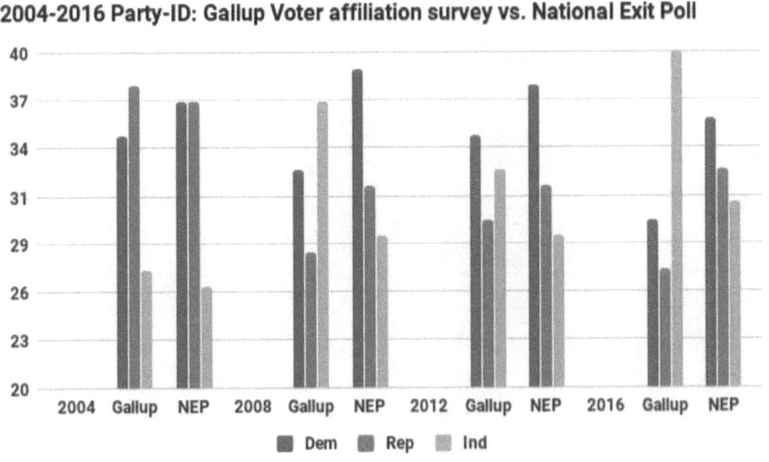

2004-2016 Party-ID: Gallup Voter affiliation survey vs. National Exit Poll

TDMS|RESEARCH

www.tdmsresearch.com

2016 PRESIDENTIAL ELECTION - EXIT POLLS VERSUS REPORTED VOTE COUNT

Presidential Election Clinton v. Trump	CNN PUBLISHED EXIT POLLS (EP) [1]				REPORTED VOTE COUNT (VC) [2]			EP / VC DISCREPANCIES	
	CLINTON EP	TRUMP EP	MARGIN TRUMP - CLINTON [3]	MOE [4] ON THE DIFFERENCE	CLINTON VC	TRUMP VC	MARGIN TRUMP - CLINTON [3]	MARGIN DISCREPANCY IN FAVOR OF TRUMP	DISCREPANCY GREATER THAN EP MOE
MISSOURI	42.8%	51.2%	8.4%	4.7%	37.88%	56.39%	18.5%	10.1%	5.4%
NEW JERSEY	59.8%	35.8%	-24.0%	5.8%	55.00%	41.02%	-14.0%	10.0%	4.2%
UTAH	32.4%	41.8%	9.4%	5.7%	27.17%	45.05%	17.9%	8.5%	2.8%
MAINE	51.2%	40.2%	-11.0%	5.0%	47.83%	44.87%	-3.0%	8.0%	3.0%
OHIO	47.0%	47.1%	0.2%	3.4%	43.24%	51.31%	8.1%	7.9%	4.5%
SOUTH CAROLINA	42.8%	50.3%	7.5%	4.9%	40.67%	54.94%	14.3%	6.7%	1.8%
NORTH CAROLINA	48.6%	46.5%	-2.0%	3.0%	46.17%	49.83%	3.7%	5.7%	2.7%
IOWA	44.1%	48.0%	3.9%	3.5%	41.74%	51.15%	9.4%	5.5%	2.0%
PENNSYLVANIA	50.5%	46.1%	-4.4%	3.8%	47.46%	48.17%	0.7%	5.1%	1.4%
NEW HAMPSHIRE	49.4%	44.2%	-5.3%	4.6%	46.83%	46.46%	-0.4%	4.9%	0.3%
WISCONSIN	48.2%	44.3%	-3.9%	3.5%	46.45%	47.22%	0.8%	4.7%	1.2%
INDIANA	39.6%	53.9%	14.3%	4.5%	37.46%	56.47%	19.0%	4.7%	0.2%
GEORGIA	46.8%	48.2%	1.4%	3.7%	45.35%	50.44%	5.1%	3.7%	
NEVADA	48.7%	42.8%	-5.9%	3.8%	47.92%	45.50%	-2.4%	3.5%	
KENTUCKY	35.0%	61.5%	26.5%	5.7%	32.68%	62.52%	29.8%	3.3%	
FLORIDA	47.7%	46.4%	-1.4%	3.0%	47.41%	48.60%	1.2%	2.5%	
VIRGINIA	50.9%	43.2%	-7.7%	3.5%	49.75%	44.43%	-5.3%	2.4%	
NEW MEXICO	47.9%	37.8%	-10.1%	4.6%	48.26%	40.04%	-8.2%	1.9%	
OREGON	50.7%	38.8%	-12.0%	5.5%	50.07%	39.09%	-11.0%	1.0%	
ARIZONA	43.6%	46.9%	3.3%	4.5%	44.58%	48.08%	3.5%	0.2%	
MICHIGAN	46.8%	46.8%	0.0%	3.6%	47.03%	47.25%	0.2%	0.2%	
COLORADO	46.5%	41.5%	-5.0%	5.0%	48.16%	43.25%	-4.9%	0.1%	
WASHINGTON	51.3%	35.8%	-15.5%	5.6%	52.54%	36.83%	-15.7%	-0.2%	
TEXAS	42.3%	51.8%	9.5%	3.7%	43.24%	52.23%	9.0%	-0.5%	
MINNESOTA	45.7%	45.8%	0.1%	4.7%	46.04%	44.87%	-1.2%	-1.3%	
CALIFORNIA	60.0%	31.5%	-28.5%	3.7%	61.48%	31.49%	-30.0%	-1.5%	
ILLINOIS	53.6%	38.4%	-15.2%	7.6%	55.25%	38.36%	-16.9%	-1.7%	
NEW YORK	55.8%	39.8%	-16.0%	5.1%	59.01%	36.52%	-22.5%	-6.5%	1.4%
NATIONAL	47.9%	44.7%	-3.2%	1.3%	48.18%	46.09%	-2.1%	1.1%	

FINAL TABLE. Table and notes by Theodore de Macedo Soares - www.tdmsresearch.com

Clinton's wins in the exit polls of four key battleground states are highlighted in blue. Trump's wins in the computer vote counts in these same states are highlighted in red. Slight apparent discrepancies in percentage arithmetic are due to rounding.

Clinton's margin in in IL, CA and NY states totaled 6.95 million. But as many as 3 million of Clinton's margin may have been fraudulent. Clinton won the national popular vote by 2.8 million votes.

She won California by 4.27 million, New York by 1.7 million and Illinois by 945,000 votes – a total of 6.9 million. Trump won the other 48 states by 4.1 million.

When Decided:	Clinton-	Trump-	Other
	IL	CA	NY
Recorded %	56-39-5	62-32-4	60-37-3
Pre Oct. 1	66-32-2	67-29-4	67-31-2
Post Oct. 1	33-55-12	51-42-7	38-53-9
Votes (mil)	5.5	14.2	7.5
Margin	0.95	4.3	1.7

Decided	Pct	Clinton	Trump	Other
Post Sept 1	40%	42.0%	48.0%	10.0%
Pre- Sept 1	60%	52.5%	45.0%	2.5%
Total	100%	48.3%	46.2%	5.5

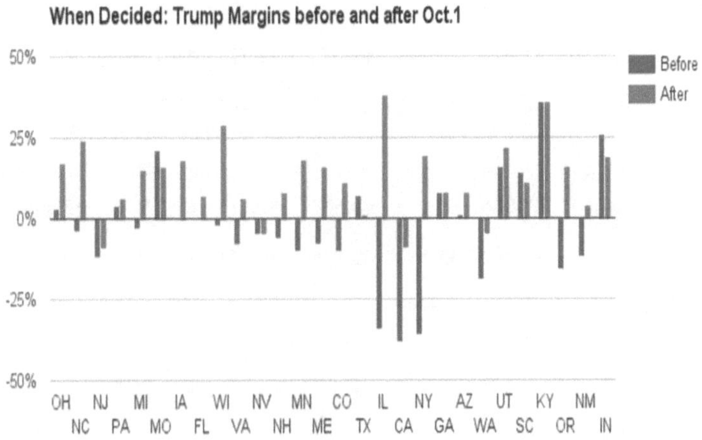

Clinton won the 28 unadjusted state exit polls by 49.6-43.6% and the corresponding recorded vote by 49.2-45.2%. But Independents outnumbered Democrats by 6.7%. Trump won Independents by 7.7% over Clinton. In the 23 states not exit polled, Trump won the recorded vote: 50.4-43.7%

The Final National Exit Poll was forced to match the recorded vote. Clinton won the recorded vote by 48.3-46.2% and the National Exit Poll by 47.7-46.2%. Trump won Independents by just 46-42% – a 5.8% discrepancy from the pre-election polls that he led by 9.8%. Trump won the average Gallup-adjusted poll by 44.4-42.9% and Independents by 43.6-33.8%.

	Votes	Unadj EPoll		Reported		Gallup adjusted	
		Clinton	Trump	Clinton	Trump	Clinton	Trump
28 states	110,702	54,875	48,233	54,509	49,999	50,664	52,776
		49.57%	43.57%	49.24%	45.17%	45.77%	47.67%
Margin			6,642		4,510		2,112
23 states	25,350	11,079	12,777	11,079	12,777	11,079	12,777
		43.71%	50.40%	43.71%	50.40%	43.71%	50.40%
Total	136,051	65,955	61,011	65,588	62,776	61,744	65,554
		48.48%	44.84%	48.21%	46.14%	45.38%	48.18%
Total margin			4,944		2,812		3,810

Sensitivity Analysis

State-adjusted Gallup National Party-ID

True Vote Model 1
Clinton Trump EV
48.1% 45.6% 197 (28 exit poll states)
43.7% 50.4% 82 (23 other states)
47.3% 46.5% 279

True Vote Model 2:
Scenario 1: Undecided Voters to Trump: 50%
Clinton Trump EV
45.5% 46.8% 224 (28 exit poll states)
43.7% 50.4% 82 (23 other states)
45.1% 47.5% 306

Scenario 2: Undecided Voters to Trump: 60%
Clinton Trump EV
45.0% 47.3% 231 (28 exit poll states)
43.7% 50.4% 82 (23 other states)
44.7% 47.9% 313

Scenario 3: Undecided Voters to Trump: 70%
Clinton Trump EV
44.5% 47.8% 260 (28 exit poll states)
43.7% 50.4% 82 (23 other states)
44.3% 48.3% 342

Four Election Scenarios: Gallup vs. National Exit Poll

1. Gallup Party-ID and True Vote Model (TVM) vote shares
2. Gallup Party-ID and National Exit Poll (NEP) vote shares
3. NEP Party-ID and NEP vote shares
4. NEP Party-ID and TVM vote shares

It is a FACT: the Reported vote is NEVER equal to the True Vote. The pundits always brainwash the public into assuming that the Reported vote represents True voter intent.

The **National Exit Poll** is always forced to match the Reported vote (Scenario 3).
NEP Party-ID is 36D-33R-31I.

Clinton leads Trump by 2.03 million votes: 47.7-46.2%.
Others (including Johnson and Stein) have just 6.1% combined. Stein has 1%.

The **True Vote Model** (Scenario 1): Gallup Party-ID: 40I-32D-28R. Trump leads Clinton by 2.18 million votes: 45.7-44.0%. How many voted for Jill Stein? Surely more than 1%.

It is clear that the third party vote is a key factor. Jill Stein had an implausibly low 1% share. Where did her votes go?

Compare Trump's 2.18 million True Vote margin in Scenario 1, in which third parties had 10.3%, to his negative margins in scenarios 2 and 3 where third parties had 6-7%. The differential indicates that Stein did better than 1%. Her votes were stolen.

1. Gallup/TVM	Party-ID	Clinton	Trump	Other
Dem	32%	89%	9%	2%
Rep	28%	7%	**90%**	3%
Ind	40%	34%	**44%**	22%
TVM Total	**100%**	**44.0%**	**45.7%**	**10.3%**
Votes (mil)	**133.26**	**58.69**	**60.87**	**13.70**

2. Gallup/NEP	Party-ID	Clinton	Trump	Other
Dem	32%	89%	8%	3%
Rep	28%	8%	88%	4%
Ind	40%	42%	46%	12%
Total	**100%**	**47.5%**	**45.6%**	**6.9%**
Votes (mil)	**133.26**	**63.33**	**60.77**	**9.17**

3. NEP/NEP	Party-ID	Clinton	Trump	Other
Dem	36%	89%	8%	3%
Rep	33%	8%	88%	4%
Ind	31%	42%	46%	12%
Total	**100%**	**47.7%**	**46.2%**	**6.1%**
Votes (mil)	**133.26**	**63.57**	**61.54**	**8.16**

4. NEP/TVM	Party-ID	Clinton	Trump	Other
Dem	36%	89%	9%	2%
Rep	33%	7%	90%	3%
Ind	31%	34%	44%	22%
Total	**100%**	**44.9%**	**46.6%**	**8.5%**
Votes (mil)	**133.26**	**59.82**	**62.07**	**11.37**

Sensitivity Analysis

		DJT	% Rep		
DJT	86.0%	88.0%	**90.0%**	92.0%	94.0%
%Ind			**DJT**		
48%	46.2%	46.7%	47.3%	47.8%	48.4%
44%	44.6%	45.1%	**45.7%**	46.2%	46.8%
40%	43.0%	43.5%	44.1%	44.6%	45.2%
			HRC		
48%	43.6%	43.0%	42.4%	41.9%	41.3%
44%	45.2%	44.6%	**44.0%**	43.5%	42.9%
40%	46.8%	46.2%	45.6%	45.1%	44.5%
			Vote Marg		
48%	3.5	5.0	6.4	7.9	9.4
44%	-0.8	0.7	**2.2**	3.7	5.2
40%	-5.1	-3.6	-2.1	-0.6	0.9

Chapter 6: True Vote Calculations

True Vote Model I: Adjusted Party-ID and Returning 2012 voters
True Vote Model II: Exit Poll Party-ID vs. Gallup Voter affiliation

Methodology
National Party-ID crosstab is the basis for the analysis. Independent vote shares were adjusted to force a match to the total exit poll shares.

True Vote Calculation
Party-ID is based on the Gallup National Voter Affiliation survey.
Method 1- Reported vote shares (CNN).
Method 2- Vote shares calculated in the Election Model.

Summary (28 states)
Unadjusted exit polls: Clinton leads 47.6-44.6% (unweighted average)
Party-ID: 35.1D – 32.7R – 32.2I
Share of Independents: Clinton 44.0-Trump 40.6% (not plausible)

Reported Vote (CNN)
Trump 47.3-46.7% (unweighted average)
Party-ID: 35.1D – 32.7R – 32.2I
Share of Independents: Trump 48.0-Clinton 40.3% (plausible)

True Vote
Model 1: Trump 46.7-46.0% (unweighted, reported vote shares)
Model 2: Trump 48.4-43.8% (unweighted, Election Model shares)
Party-ID: 32.0D – 29.3R – 38.7I

9 National Pre-Election Polls	Gallup	Clinton	Trump	Johnson	Stein
Ind	40.0%	33.8%	43.6%	8.9%	3.8%
Dem	32.0%	88.1%	6.9%	1.3%	1.7%
Rep	28.0%	5.6%	87.8%	3.9%	0.3%
Pre-UVA	94.7%	43.3%	44.2%	5.1%	2.1%
Votes	128,963	55,792	57,007	6,540	2,757
EVote	538	232	306		
Adjusted		44.4%	47.6%	5.1%	2.1%
Votes	136,216	60,471	64,836	6,908	2,912
Evote	538	182	356		

9 Polls	NEP	Clinton	Trump	Johnson	Stein
Ind	31.0%	33.8%	43.6%	8.9%	3.8%
Dem	36.0%	88.1%	6.9%	1.3%	1.7%
Rep	33.0%	5.6%	87.8%	3.9%	0.3%
Pre-UVA	95.3%	44.0%	44.9%	4.5%	1.9%
Votes	129,914	57,194	58,395	5,871	2,444
EVote	538	212	326		
Adjusted		45.0%	47.8%	4.5%	1.9%
Votes	136,216	61,271	65,137	6,155	2,562
Evote	538	216	327		

		Unadj Exit Poll		CNN poll (Reported vote)		Party-ID Gallup Survey TVM1		TVM 2	
	Votes	Clinton	Trump	Clinton	Trump	Clinton	Trump	Clinton	Trump
Avg	110,702	47.5%	44.5%	46.6%	46.7%	45.4%	47.3%	43.3%	47.7%
Wtd Avg		49.5%	43.5%	49.3%	45.2%	48.0%	45.8%	44.6%	46.0%
1 OH	5,496	47.0%	47.1%	43.6%	51.7%	43.9%	51.1%	43.2%	50.1%
2 NC	4,742	48.6%	46.5%	46.2%	49.8%	47.3%	48.1%	46.2%	46.3%
3 NJ	3,907	59.8%	35.8%	55.0%	41.0%	53.6%	42.3%	45.1%	46.1%
4 PA	5,950	50.5%	46.1%	47.9%	48.6%	49.9%	45.7%	47.9%	45.6%
5 MI	4,799	46.8%	46.8%	47.3%	47.5%	44.8%	49.3%	45.4%	47.1%
6 MO	2,809	42.8%	51.2%	38.1%	56.8%	37.2%	57.1%	41.9%	51.4%
7 IA	1,566	44.1%	48.0%	41.7%	51.1%	40.6%	50.4%	41.0%	52.1%
8 FL	9,420	47.7%	46.4%	47.8%	49.0%	47.7%	49.2%	44.4%	48.0%
9 WI	2,976	48.2%	44.3%	46.5%	47.2%	46.9%	46.4%	43.6%	47.4%
10 VA	3,983	50.9%	43.2%	49.8%	44.4%	45.1%	48.1%	42.1%	48.4%
11 NV	1,125	48.7%	42.8%	47.9%	45.5%	45.6%	47.3%	44.0%	47.1%
12 NH	742	49.4%	44.2%	47.0%	46.6%	46.2%	46.9%	40.3%	51.1%
13 MN	2,945	45.7%	45.8%	46.4%	44.9%	46.8%	45.2%	44.5%	46.5%
14 ME	748	51.2%	40.2%	47.8%	44.9%	46.5%	45.2%	43.0%	48.6%
15 CO	2,780	46.5%	41.5%	48.2%	43.3%	44.1%	47.0%	40.5%	48.9%
16 TX	8,969	42.3%	51.8%	43.2%	52.2%	45.0%	50.0%	41.7%	50.9%
17 IL	5,536	53.6%	38.4%	55.8%	38.8%	52.9%	40.7%	47.2%	45.7%
18 CA	14,182	60.0%	31.5%	61.7%	31.6%	57.0%	34.8%	47.0%	32.1%
19 NY	7,456	55.8%	39.8%	59.6%	36.7%	58.6%	36.0%	51.5%	43.5%
20 GA	4,115	46.8%	48.2%	45.6%	50.8%	44.7%	51.5%	42.6%	52.6%
21 AZ	2,573	43.6%	46.9%	45.1%	48.7%	44.6%	48.8%	39.6%	50.7%
22 WA	3,184	51.3%	35.8%	54.7%	38.4%	49.0%	44.5%	43.6%	48.1%
23 UT	1,131	32.4%	41.8%	27.5%	45.5%	27.5%	45.8%	27.4%	45.6%
24 SC	2,103	42.8%	50.3%	40.7%	54.9%	47.2%	48.1%	41.8%	51.1%
25 KY	1,924	35.0%	61.5%	32.7%	62.5%	26.9%	66.2%	41.0%	48.8%
26 OR	2,001	50.7%	38.8%	50.1%	39.1%	49.8%	40.2%	45.7%	43.6%
27 NM	798	47.9%	37.8%	48.3%	40.0%	47.0%	40.4%	47.7%	43.9%
28 IN	2,741	39.6%	53.9%	37.9%	56.8%	35.9%	57.8%	41.5%	53.6%

The True Vote Model- Returning Voters

Exit pollsters no longer ask: *Who did you vote for in the previous election?* However we can approximate the crosstab by calculating the vote shares required to match the total recorded vote.

The 2008 presidential election was the last one in which the National (NEP) and state exit polls asked "**HOW DID YOU VOTE IN THE LAST ELECTION?**" The question provided clear proof of fraud in all elections from 1988-2008. The crosstab required more returning Bush voters than were still alive in order to match the bogus recorded vote in 1992 (119% turnout), 2004 (110%) and 2008 (103%).

National Exit Poll assumptions (match recorded vote)
Equal 96% turnout of living 2012 Obama and Romney voters.
Clinton wins 88% of returning Obama and 7% of Romney voters.
Trump wins 7% of returning Obama and 90% of Romney voters.
Trump and Clinton split new voters 44-47%.

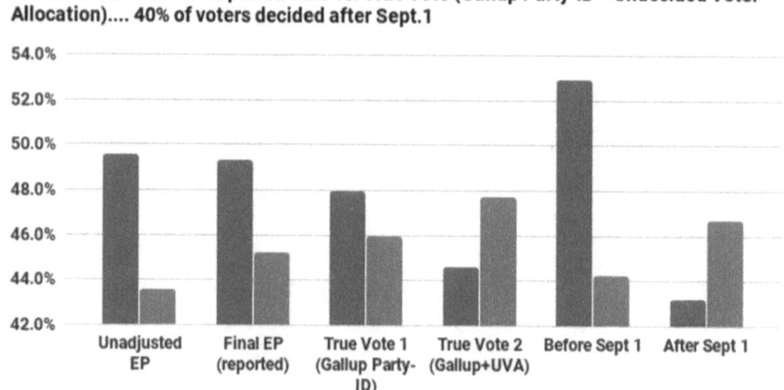

% of Ind (Clinton-Trump): Unadj EP 44.0-41.2%; Reported 42.3-47.4%

National Exit Poll

2012	Mix	Clinton	Trump	Other
Obama	44.12%	88%	7%	5%
Romney	40.80%	6%	90%	4%
Other	1.54%	45%	45%	10%
DNV (new)	13.54%	46.4%	41.9%	11.7%
	Recorded share	48.25%	46.17%	5.58%
	Recorded Vote	65.72	62.90	7.60
	Margin	2.83		

True Vote Model

2012	Mix	Clinton	Trump	Other
Obama	41.33%	85%	7%	8%
Romney	40.80%	6%	90%	4%
Other	1.54%	45%	45%	10%
DNV (new)	16.32%	45%	45%	10%
	True Vote share	45.62%	47.65%	6.73%
	True Vote	62.14	64.91	9.16
	Margin		2.77	

Sensitivity: Trump's shares of returning Obama and Romney voters

			% Obama		
Trump	5%	6%	7%	8%	9%
% Romney			Trump		
92%	47.6%	48.1%	48.5%	48.9%	49.3%
91%	47.2%	47.6%	48.1%	48.5%	48.9%
90%	46.8%	47.2%	**47.6%**	48.1%	48.5%
89%	46.4%	46.8%	47.2%	47.7%	48.1%
88%	46.0%	46.4%	46.8%	47.3%	47.7%
			Clinton		
92%	45.6%	45.2%	44.8%	44.4%	44.0%
91%	46.0%	45.6%	45.2%	44.8%	44.4%
90%	46.4%	46.0%	**45.6%**	45.2%	44.8%
89%	46.9%	46.4%	46.0%	45.6%	45.2%
88%	47.3%	46.9%	46.4%	46.0%	45.6%
			Margin		
92%	2.0%	2.8%	3.7%	4.5%	5.3%
91%	1.2%	2.0%	2.8%	3.7%	4.5%
90%	0.4%	1.2%	2.0%	2.9%	3.7%
89%	-0.4%	0.4%	1.2%	2.0%	2.9%
88%	-1.3%	-0.4%	0.4%	1.2%	2.1%
			Margin		
92%	2.74	3.86	4.99	6.12	7.24
91%	1.63	2.75	3.88	5.00	6.13
90%	0.51	1.64	2.77	3.89	5.02
89%	-0.60	0.53	1.66	2.78	3.91
88%	-1.71	-0.58	0.54	1.67	2.80

Chapter 7: California and Humboldt County

Clinton won the recorded vote: 61.7-31.6% (4.27 million votes). Consider that in 2012, Obama beat Romney by 60.2-37.1% (3.0 million votes) in California. Did Clinton really beat Obama's margin by 1.2 million? To match the recorded vote, Clinton needed to win new voters by 90-2%. Nearly 450,000 angry Sanders voters did not turn out for Hillary.

Clinton won the True Vote by 55.0-37.8% (2.44 million votes). The 1.8 million True Vote discrepancy from the recorded vote comprised nearly 2/3 of her bogus 2.8 million vote national margin.

Media shills insist that Clinton won by 3 million votes. It has become their Mantra, along with the debunked Russian "collusion". Show them the numbers and tell them: THE RECORDED VOTE IS NEVER EQUAL TO THE TRUE VOTE. THERE IS NO SUCH THING AS A FRAUD-FREE ELECTION.

How did Clinton win the state by 4.27 million votes? She won the national recorded vote by 2.8 million, so Trump won the other states by at least 1.5 million (conservative).

Clinton did 7.0% better in CA than Obama in 2012. Clinton won by 61.7-31.6%, a 30.1% margin (4.27 million votes). Obama won by 60.2-37.1%, a 23.1% margin (3.01 million votes). If Clinton's margin was 23.1%, she would have won by 3.3 million votes. In the CNN final CA exit poll (matched to the reported vote), the Party-ID is 47D-23R-30I

Was Clinton more popular than Obama? Not plausible.

When the CA final exit poll Party-ID is adjusted from 47D-23R-30I to 34.2D-22.3R-43.5I based on the change in national Party ID from 2014, Clinton wins CA by 56.1-36.5% (2.78 million votes).

Humboldt County, CA is the only county in the U.S. which uses Open Source software to count and audit votes. In the CA primary, Sanders had his highest vote share (71%) in Humboldt. Jill Stein also had her highest share (6.2%) in Humboldt.

Is it just a coincidence that Bernie and Jill both had their highest vote shares in Humboldt? Or was it due to the foolproof Open Source voting system?

Hillary had 56% in Humboldt, nearly 6% lower than her total CA share. It is a fact that Bernie was cheated in CA by massive fraud. Who is to say that Hillary did not also cheat in CA to pad her popular vote margin?

California True Vote Model- Party-ID

Exit Poll	Pct	Clinton	Trump	Johnson	Stein	Other
Dem	47%	92%	5%	1%	1%	1%
Rep	23%	13%	84%	2%	1%	0%
Ind	30%	46%	33%	7%	5%	9%
Match	100%	60.0%	31.6%	3.0%	2.2%	3%
Unadjusted	100%	60.0%	31.5%	2.0%	1.3%	5%
Votes	14,182	8,509	4,467	284	184	737
	Margin	-4,042	-28.5%			

Recorded	Pct	Clinton	Trump	Johnson	Stein	Other
Dem	47%	92%	5%	1%	1%	1%
Rep	23%	13%	84%	2%	1%	0%
Ind	30%	50%	37%	7%	5%	1%
Match	100%	61.2%	32.8%	3.0%	2.2%	0.8%
Recorded	**100%**	**61.7%**	**31.6%**	**3.4%**	**2.0%**	**1.3%**
Votes	14,182	8,754	4,484	479	279	187
	Margin	-4,270	-30.1%			

TRUE	Gallup	Clinton	Trump	Johnson	Stein	Other
Dem	34.2%	92%	5%	1%	1%	1%
Rep	22.3%	13%	84%	2%	1%	0%
Ind	43.5%	50%	37%	7%	5%	1%
TVM	**100%**	**56.1%**	**36.5%**	**3.8%**	**2.7%**	**0.8%**
Votes	14,182	7,958	5,182	544	389	110
	Margin	-2,776	-4.7%			

California True Vote Model: Returning Voters

Recorded

2012	Pct	Clinton	Trump	Other	
Obama	50.5%	90.0%	6.0%	4.0%	
Romney	31.1%	5.0%	88.0%	7.0%	
Other	2.2%	20.0%	20.0%	60.0%	
DNV (new)	16.2%	88.4%	4.7%	7.0%	Margin
Recorded		**61.73%**	**31.62%**	**6.7%**	**30.1%**
Votes	14,181,595	8,753,904	4,484,595	943,096	4,269,309
Unadj EP		60.0%	31.5%	8.5%	28.5%

TRUE VOTE

2012	Pct	Clinton	Trump	Other	
Obama	47.3%	90.0%	6.0%	4.0%	
Romney	31.1%	5.0%	88.0%	7.0%	
Other	2.2%	20.0%	20.0%	60.0%	
DNV (new)	19.3%	56.0%	35.0%	9.0%	Margin
True Vote		**55.4%**	**37.4%**	**7.1%**	**18.0%**
Votes	14,181,595	7,859,128	5,309,796	1,012,670	2,549,332
Recorded		61.7%	31.62%	6.65%	30.1%

Humboldt County

Humboldt County, CA is the only county in the U.S. which uses an Open Source System (TEVS) to count and audit votes. The system was installed in 2006.

In the CA primary, Bernie Sanders had his highest share (71%) in Humboldt. In the 2016 presidential election, Jill Stein's 6.1% Humboldt share was her highest in the state – just like it was for Bernie. Clinton's 56% share in Humboldt ranked #20 of 58 California counties.

Stein's average in the 19 counties was 2.3%. Clinton averaged 68.0%. So how come Stein did 4% better in Humboldt than she did in the other 19 liberal counties? And Clinton 12% worse?

Did Jill Stein actually have an approximate 6% True vote in liberal CA? Did she have 4% nationally? Who believes that she had just 1%? Could it be that fraud was prevented in Humboldt? Were nearly 2/3 of Stein's votes blue-shifted to Clinton? Was Clinton's 61% CA share inflated by at least 4%? Note that 4% of 14 million CA votes is 560,000. That's a 1.2 million difference in vote margin. She won the national recorded vote by 2.8 million.

In 2008-2012, Obama did 2.58% better in Humboldt than he did in the state. This is to be expected. But in 2016, Clinton did 1.75% worse in Humboldt while her 4.26% increase over Obama in CA represents a 1.2 million increase in vote margin. This is counter-intuitive. How did Clinton get all those votes? Was she really that popular? Or was her vote padded?

There is always election fraud. But in Humboldt, we can assume that the recorded vote is the True Vote due to its near foolproof Open Source system. There is no reason to believe Clinton's recorded CA vote is legitimate.

Election Transparency Project (ETP) The ETP is a documented case in which technology uncovered vote miscounts. Volunteers scanned ballots after the election to verify the integrity of the Diebold/Premier machines. The images were made publicly available and used TEV's ballot counting software.

They found that 197 ballots were deleted by the Diebold/Premier GEMS software used by Humboldt County to tally the vote. This software glitch resulted in the certification of inaccurate election results. The Election Administration Research Center at UC Berkeley site contains ballot images that were scanned during this project (the same images can also be obtained on DVD from the Elections Office).The ballot extraction code reads the ballot image and uses OCR to automatically determine the candidates listed on the ballot. It reads the images and stores the results in a database.

The ETP is overseen by officials from the Humboldt County Elections Office. However, the "elbow grease" of this project, with a couple of exceptions, is done by volunteers who care about the integrity of our elections. These volunteers, working on weekends, holidays, and evenings, use a high-end office scanner to scan all paper ballots cast in an election. The scanner produces digital images of the ballots. The ballots are "digitally signed" to mark their authenticity and uploaded to the Internet for distribution. These images are also available on DVD at the Elections Office. One notable feature is that each ballot is imprinted with a unique serial number before it is imaged. Part of the serial number contains information about on the box the ballot comes from. This feature "ties together" an image on the Internet with the paper ballot.

A site belonging to ETP volunteer Mitch Trachtenberg contains an Open Source software program that automates the counting of these ballot images. This auditing tool is quite valuable in producing a tally that can be used to compare against the results produced by software that is not subject to inspection by members of the general public. In short, this tool alleviates the need of counting ballots by hand and does so in a transparent manner.

Humboldt Democratic 2-party share

1988-2004 Before TEVS: 57.2%

2008-2016 After TEVS: 64.6%

California Presidential share

	Dem	Rep	Other	
2008	60.21%	36.46%	3.33%	
2012	60.24%	37.12%	2.64%	
2016	**61.73%**	**31.62%**	**6.66%**	**HRC margin 7% higher than Obama?**

Humboldt Presidential share

	Dem	Rep	Other
2008	62.05%	33.95%	.4.00%
2012	59.68%	32.61%	7.72%
2016	**56.04%**	**31.01%**	**12.95%**

Democratic 2-party Presidential share

	CA	Humboldt	.Diff	
2008	62.28%	64.64%	2.36%	
2012	61.87%	64.67%	2.80%	
2016	**66.13%**	**64.37%**	**-1.75%**	**< HRC gains 4.26% over Obama?**

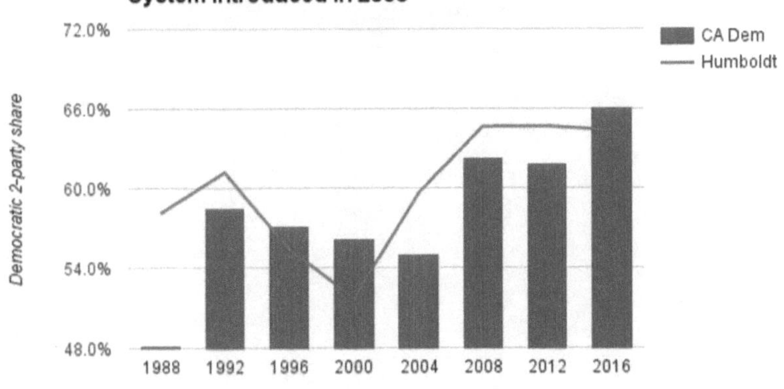

Stein's average in the 19 counties was 2.3%. Clinton averaged 68.0%. So how come Stein did 4% better in Humboldt than she did in the other 19 liberal counties? And Clinton 12% worse?

```
...................... Stein Clinton
1 San Francisco.. 2.4% 85.0%
2 Alameda......... 2.7  78.7
3 Marin..............2.2  78.1
4 San Mateo........1.6  75.7
5 Santa Cruz.......3.5  73.9
6 Santa Clara......1.8  72.7
7 Los Angeles......2.2  71.8
8 Sonoma...........3.2  69.4
9 Contra Costa.....1.9  68.5
10 Imperial..........1.6  67.9
11 Monterey.........2.1  66.8
12 Yolo..............2.2 66.7
13 Napa.............2.1  63.9
14 Solano...........1.7  61.6
15 Santa Barbara .2.1  60.6
16 Mendocino.......5.6  58.9
17 Sacramento.....1.8  58.3
18 San Benito......1.7 57.1
19 San Diego.......1.8 56.3
20 Humboldt........6.2 56.0
```

	California	Votes	Stein	Clinton	Trump	Johnson	Other	Margin
1	Alameda	654,266	2.7%	78.7%	14.7%	2.6%	1.3%	418,920
2	Alpine	602	3.5%	55.5%	36.1%	4.2%	0.8%	117
3	Amador	17,734	1.3%	33.9%	59.1%	4.5%	1.2%	-4,481
4	Butte	95,564	2.7%	43.5%	47.2%	4.8%	1.7%	-3,577
5	Calaveras	23,136	1.8%	34.3%	58.4%	4.8%	0.7%	-5,567
6	Colusa	6,632	1.3%	40.1%	53.5%	3.9%	1.1%	-890
7	Contra Costa	466,175	1.9%	68.5%	24.9%	3.5%	1.3%	203,331
8	Del Norte	9,558	2.6%	36.5%	53.7%	4.4%	2.9%	-1,649
9	El Dorado	93,591	1.5%	38.9%	52.6%	5.4%	1.6%	-12,843
10	Fresno	282,319	1.5%	50.1%	43.9%	3.3%	1.2%	17,292
11	Glenn	9,470	1.0%	32.4%	61.1%	4.0%	1.5%	-2,723
12	**Humboldt**	**59,246**	**6.2%**	**56.0%**	**31.0%**	**3.7%**	**3.1%**	**14,827**
13	Imperial	48,091	1.6%	67.9%	26.4%	2.5%	1.6%	19,963
14	Inyo	8,086	2.7%	39.0%	52.5%	4.1%	1.7%	-1,093
15	Kern	244,163	1.2%	40.4%	53.1%	3.8%	1.5%	-30,895
16	Kings	33,915	1.2%	40.2%	53.4%	4.0%	1.3%	-4,476
17	Lake	24,496	3.8%	46.9%	43.3%	4.5%	1.5%	897
18	Lassen	10,524	1.0%	21.1%	72.0%	4.5%	1.4%	-5,350
19	Los Angeles	3,434,308	2.2%	71.8%	22.4%	2.6%	1.0%	1,694,621
20	Madera	43,112	1.5%	39.5%	54.2%	3.6%	1.2%	-6,328
21	Marin	139,273	2.2%	78.1%	15.6%	3.0%	1.1%	86,936
22	Mariposa	8,877	2.1%	35.2%	58.4%	3.7%	0.6%	-2,063
23	Mendocino	37,477	5.6%	58.9%	29.1%	3.6%	2.9%	11,191
24	Merced	70,789	1.7%	52.7%	40.6%	3.4%	1.6%	8,592

25	Modoc	3,788	1.3%	23.2%	71.2%	3.2%	1.1%	-1,819
26	Mono	5,276	2.7%	52.6%	40.0%	4.2%	0.5%	662
27	Monterey	133,408	2.1%	66.8%	26.2%	3.4%	1.5%	54,193
28	Napa	61,372	2.1%	63.9%	28.4%	4.2%	1.5%	21,788
29	Nevada	54,935	4.0%	47.4%	42.5%	4.3%	1.7%	2,688
30	Orange	1,197,521	1.5%	50.9%	42.4%	3.9%	1.4%	102,813
31	Placer	182,839	1.4%	40.2%	52.0%	5.1%	1.3%	-21,629
32	Plumas	9,676	1.9%	35.8%	56.0%	4.3%	2.1%	-1,961
33	Riverside	751,391	1.5%	49.7%	44.4%	3.2%	1.2%	40,452
34	Sacramento	559,330	1.8%	58.3%	33.9%	4.4%	1.7%	136,234
35	San Benito	21,924	1.7%	57.1%	35.8%	3.7%	1.8%	4,680
36	San Bernardino	653,983	1.6%	52.1%	41.5%	3.2%	1.6%	69,593
37	San Diego	1,306,400	1.8%	56.3%	36.6%	4.0%	1.4%	257,710
38	San Francisco	405,792	2.4%	85.0%	9.3%	2.2%	1.0%	307,396
39	San Joaquin	224,166	1.4%	54.0%	39.7%	3.6%	1.3%	32,188
40	San Luis Obispo	135,009	2.1%	49.7%	41.6%	4.8%	1.8%	10,943
41	San Mateo	314,384	1.6%	75.7%	18.4%	3.0%	1.3%	179,953
42	Santa Barbara	176,786	2.1%	60.6%	31.9%	3.8%	1.6%	50,777
43	Santa Clara	703,709	1.8%	72.7%	20.6%	3.6%	1.3%	366,858
44	Santa Cruz	128,821	3.5%	73.9%	17.4%	3.4%	1.8%	72,811
45	Shasta	80,053	1.6%	27.9%	64.7%	4.2%	1.6%	-29,477
46	Sierra	1,830	2.3%	32.8%	57.3%	5.4%	2.2%	-447
47	Siskiyou	20,492	2.8%	35.3%	55.3%	4.3%	2.3%	-4,107
48	Solano	166,113	1.7%	61.6%	31.3%	3.8%	1.7%	50,440
49	Sonoma	231,253	3.2%	69.4%	22.2%	3.9%	1.3%	109,027

50	Stanislaus	172,146	1.5%	47.4%	45.6%	3.9%	1.6%	3,153
51	Sutter	33,523	1.1%	39.0%	54.2%	4.3%	1.3%	-5,100
52	Tehama	23,908	1.2%	28.5%	64.8%	4.0%	1.5%	-8,685
53	Trinity	5,686	4.2%	38.9%	49.5%	5.3%	2.1%	-598
54	Tulare	112,334	1.4%	42.4%	51.9%	3.4%	0.9%	-10,714
55	Tuolumne	25,529	1.5%	35.7%	57.0%	4.3%	1.5%	-5,428
56	Ventura	351,726	1.8%	55.3%	37.6%	3.9%	1.4%	62,079
57	Yolo	82,090	2.2%	66.7%	25.3%	4.1%	1.8%	34,013
58	Yuba	22,998	1.9%	34.4%	57.3%	4.6%	1.8%	-5,260

Chapter 8: Election Fraud Components

This analysis shows the effect of adjustments to the recorded vote (estimated illegals, disenfranchised/cross-checked, vote flipping) and corresponding changes to the National Exit Poll (NEP) Race category. According to the 2016 Census, 87.3% of registered voters turned out.

Scenario 1:

- 1 million voters were disenfranchised due to Cross-check
- 1.3 million additional voters were disenfranchised
- 1 million illegal voters

Clinton had 80% of illegal and disenfranchised voters
3.2 million votes (4.8%) were flipped on voting machines from Trump to Clinton.
0.6 million third party votes flipped to Clinton.

Of the 137.5 million votes cast, there were 1.3= 1.0+1.3-1.0 million uncounted votes.

Trump is a winner by 3.3 million votes (48.2-45.8%}

		Clinton	Trump	Other
Illegal	1.0	80%	15%	5%
Disenfranchised	2.3	80%	5%	5%
Vote Flip	4.0	5%	80%	15%

Adjustments				
Recorded	136.2	65.7	62.9	7.6
Illegal		-0.80	-0.15	-0.05
Disenfranchised		1.84	0.35	0.12
Net Vote Flip		-3.80	3.20	0.60

Adjusted				
Votes	137.5	63.0	66.3	8.2
Share		45.8%	48.2%	6.0%

National Exit Poll (Census adjustments)

Race	Pct	Clinton	Trump	Other
White	73.30%	34.7%	58.9%	6.4%
Black	12.45%	89%	8%	3%
Latino	9.22%	66%	28%	6%
Asian	3.67%	65%	27%	8%
Other	1.36%	56%	36%	8%
Adjusted	**100%**	**45.8%**	**48.2%**	**6.0%**
Recorded	100%	48.3%	46.2%	5.6%

Race: Census and share of Whites matched to the adjusted vote

Race	Census Pct	Clinton	Trump	Other
White	73.32%	34.7%	58.9%	6.4%
Black	12.45%	89%	8%	3%
Latino	9.22%	66%	28%	6%
Asian	3.67%	65%	27%	8%
Other	1.36%	56%	36%	8%
Adj Share	**100.0%**	**45.78%**	**48.20%**	**6.02%**
Votes	**137.52**	**62.96**	**66.28**	**8.27**
Recorded	100.0%	48.25%	46.17%	5.59%

Sensitivity Analysis

Vote Flip to Clinton	70.0%	Illegal 80.0%	90.0%
		Trump	
3.0%	48.2%	48.3%	48.3%
5.0%	48.1%	**48.20%**	48.3%
7.0%	48.1%	48.1%	48.2%
		Clinton	
3.0%	45.8%	45.7%	45.7%
5.0%	45.9%	**45.78%**	45.7%
7.0%	45.9%	45.8%	45.8%
		Trump	
3.0%	66.26	66.36	66.46
5.0%	66.18	**66.28**	66.38
7.0%	66.10	66.20	66.30
		Margin	
3.0%	3.28	3.48	3.68
5.0%	3.12	**3.33**	3.52
7.0%	2.96	3.17	3.36

Scenario 2:

Base case assumptions
1) Illegals: 80% of 1 million for Clinton
2) Uncounted: 80% of 7 million disenfranchised for Clinton
3) Voting machines: 4.1 million to Trump and 0.5 3rd-party votes to Clinton

Adjustments to the Recorded Vote

Assumption	Votes	to Clinton	Trump	Other
Illegal	- 1.0	80%	15%	5%
Disenfranchised.	7.0	80%	15%	5%
Net Vote Flip	5.0	8%	82%	10%
	Total	Clinton	Trump	Other
Recorded	136.22	65.72	62.89	7.61
		48.25%	46.17%	5.59%
Illegal	-1.0	-0.80	-0.15	-0.05
Disenfranchised.	7.0	5.60	1.05	0.35
Net Vote Flip	0.0	-4.60	4.10	0.50
True Vote	142.22	65.92	67.89	8.41
Share		46.35%	47.74%	5.91%

		Illegal		
Vote Flip	75.0%	80.0%		85.0%
to Clinton		Trump		
6.0%	67.94	67.99		68.04
8.0%	67.84	**67.89**		67.94
10.0%	67.74	67.79		67.84

Flip		Trump	
6.0%	47.77%	47.81%	47.84%
8.0%	47.70%	**47.74%**	47.77%
10.0%	47.63%	47.67%	47.70%

Flip		Clinton	
6.0%	46.32%	46.28%	46.25%
8.0%	46.39%	**46.35%**	46.32%
10.0%	46.46%	46.42%	46.39%

Flip		Margin	
6.0%	2.07	2.17	2.27
8.0%	1.87	**1.97**	2.07
10.0%	1.67	1.77	1.87

According to the 2016 Census, 137.5 million votes were cast (0.3% margin of error).

There were 136.2 million votes recorded, so there were 1.3 million uncounted votes.

Compare the Census (0.3% margin of error for votes cast) to the NEP. Which is closer to the truth?

	Census	MoE	NEP
White	73.30%	0.4%	71%
Black	12.45%	1.1%	12%
Latino	9.22%	1.5%	11%
Asian	3.67%	1.9%	4%
Other	1.34%	-	2%

National Exit Poll (forced to match the recorded vote)

Clinton won the recorded vote by 2.8 million votes (48.3-46.2%). Clinton won the NEP by 2.2 million votes (47.9-46.3%).

NEP	**2016**	**Clinton**	**Trump**	**Other**
White	71.0%	37%	57%	6%
Black	12.0%	89%	8%	3%
Latino	11.0%	66%	28%	6%
Asian	4.0%	65%	29%	8%
Other	2.0%	56%	36%	8%

Calculated	**100%**	**47.9%**	**46.3%**	**5.8%**
Recorded	**136,2**	**48.3%**	**46.2%**	**5.6%**

Given:
- Census 2016 registered voter turnout of 87%.
- Gallup national voter affiliation (Party-ID) on Election Day:
41% Independents, 31% Democrats and 28% Republicans
- 28 exit poll states: vote shares forced to match recorded vote.
- 23 non-exit poll states recorded vote shares.

Assumptions:
Bernie Sanders defectors:
- 5% of registered Democrats stayed home
- 4% voted for Jill Stein and 1% for Trump.

Results:
1. Adjusted Voter turnout: 78.6% Dem, 91.6% Rep, 91.6% Ind
2. Adjusted Gallup Party-ID: 29.5% Dem, 29.1% Rep, 41.4% Ind

3. Gallup Party-ID calculated for each of the 28 exit polled states

4. Trump wins by 48.13-45.33% (3.81 million votes) and 332-206 EV

Caveat: Since the final state exit poll shares were forced to match the recorded vote (and likely inflated for Clinton), Trump probably did better than indicated.

	Clinton	Trump	
28 states	45.77%	47.67%	Adjusted Exit polls
Votes	50,664	52,776	
23 states	43.71%	50.40%	Recorded vote (no exit polls)
Votes	11,079	12,777	
51 states	45.33%	48.13%	
Votes	61,744	65,554	

Voter Turnout Sensitivity

Turnout	Voted	Clinton	Trump	Johnson	Stein
95%	38.0%	40%	50%	5.0%	5.0%
89%	28.5%	88%	8%	1.0%	3.0%
95%	26.6%	7%	89%	3.0%	1.0%
93.1%	93.1%	42.1%	45.0%	3.0%	3.0%
Share	**100.0%**	**45.3%**	**48.3%**	**3.2%**	**3.2%**
Votes	**136.2**	**61.6**	**65.8**	**4.4**	**4.4**

		Trump Share			
Rep	93.0%	94.0%	95.0%	96.0%	97.0%
Dem					
87%	48.3%	48.4%	48.6%	48.7%	48.8%
88%	48.2%	48.3%	48.4%	48.6%	48.7%
89%	48.0%	48.2%	48.3%	48.4%	48.5%
90%	47.9%	48.0%	48.2%	48.3%	48.4%
91%	47.8%	47.9%	48.0%	48.2%	48.3%

		Trump			
		Votes			
Rep	93.0%	94.0%	95.0%	96.0%	97.0%
Dem					
87%	65.8	66.0	66.1	66.3	66.5
88%	65.6	65.8	66.0	66.1	66.3
89%	65.4	65.6	65.8	66.0	66.1
90%	65.2	65.4	65.6	65.8	65.9
91%	65.1	65.2	65.4	65.6	65.8

Clinton Share

Rep	93.0%	94.0%	95.0%	96.0%	97.0%
Dem					
87%	45.2%	45.1%	45.0%	44.9%	44.7%
88%	45.4%	45.3%	45.1%	45.0%	44.9%
89%	45.5%	45.4%	45.3%	45.1%	45.0%
90%	45.6%	45.5%	45.4%	45.3%	45.1%
91%	45.8%	45.6%	45.5%	45.4%	45.3%

Trump Margin

Rep	93%	94%	95%	96%	97%
Dem					
87%	3.1%	3.3%	3.6%	3.8%	4.1%
88%	2.8%	3.0%	3.3%	3.6%	3.8%
89%	2.5%	2.8%	3.0%	3.3%	3.5%
90%	2.3%	2.5%	2.8%	3.0%	3.3%
91%	2.0%	2.3%	2.5%	2.8%	3.0%

Trump Margin

Rep	93%	94%	95%	96%	97%
Dem					
87%	4.2	4.5	4.9	5.2	5.6
88%	3.8	4.1	4.5	4.8	5.2
89%	3.4	3.8	4.1	4.5	4.8
90%	3.1	3.4	3.8	4.1	4.5
91%	2.7	3.1	3.4	3.8	4.1

Note: The base case assumes that 6% of Democrats (Sanders voters) did not vote in the general election. Trump's vote margins are conservative since the calculations are based on state exit poll vote shares which were forced to match the recorded vote.

1- Trump wins base case by 328-210 EV and 1.15 million votes.
2- Trump needs 88% Rep and Dem turnout for his recorded 306 EV.
3- Clinton needs an implausible 93% turnout to win by 298-240 EV.
4- Clinton needs 92% Democratic turnout to tie Trump at 269 EV.

Dem	Rep	Ind	EV	Trump	Clinton	Margin (000)
0.85	0.92	0.87	332	64,647	62,885	1,762
0.86	0.91	0.87	328	64,347	63,195	1,152 (base case)
0.87	0.90	0.87	321	64,047	63,505	542
0.88	0.89	0.87	315	63,747	63,815	-68
0.89	0.88	0.87	305	63,447	64,125	-678
0.90	0.87	0.87	289	63,147	64,435	-1,288
0.91	0.86	0.87	289	62,847	64,745	-1,899
0.92	0.85	0.87	269	62,546	65,055	-2,509
0.93	0.84	0.87	240	62,246	65,365	-3,119

Electoral Vote Sensitivity to Registered Voter Turnout

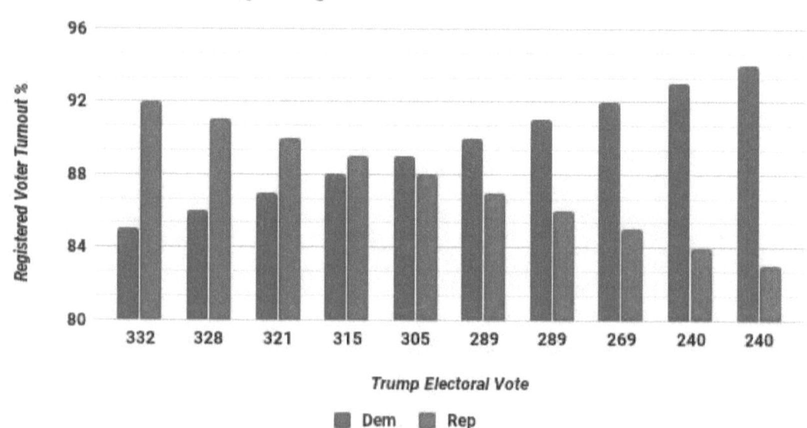

There is evidence that **millions of illegals probably voted in 2016**. According to Greg Palast, at least one million Democratic minority voters were disenfranchised via **Crosscheck** which eliminated voters with duplicate names from voter rolls. He claims that 7 million minority voters were disenfranchised.

George Soros , a Clinton backer, controls voting machines in 16 states. **Fraction Magic** is an algorithm used to flip votes on Central tabulators.
Given the Recorded vote in millions:
Clinton 65.7, Trump 62.9, Other 7.6

The Daily Caller has uncovered that George Soros, and many of the top brass in his Open Society Foundation, are deeply connected to U.K.-based voting technology company Smartmatic. Smartmatic has control over voting machines in 16 US states including contested battleground states like Arizona, Colorado, Florida, Michigan, Nevada, Pennsylvania and Virginia. Other states include California, District of Columbia, Illinois, Louisiana, Missouri, New Jersey, Oregon, Washington and Wisconsin.

In 2005, Smartmatic bought-out California-based Sequoia Voting Systems and entered the world of U.S. elections. According to Smarmatic's website, "In less than one year Smartmatic tripled Sequoia's market share" and "has offered technology and support services to the Electoral Commissions of 307 counties in 16 States."

"In 2006, Smartmatic signed what at the moment was the largest election automation contract in US history." Cook County includes Chicago and its suburbs, a geographic zone that has historically and lately been subject to criticism for voter fraud.

The chairman of Smartmatic is Lord Mark Malloch-Brown, who sits in the British House of Lords and on the board of George Soros's Open Society Foundations. He was formerly the vice-chairman of Soros's Investment Funds and the deputy secretary-general of the United Nations when he worked as chief of staff to Kofi Annan.

Malloch-Brown's resume includes stints as vice-president of the UN World Bank and in British Prime Minister Gordon Brown's cabinet. In addition to a close relationship with Soros, Malloch-Brown has worked with consulting firms that are well-connected to Bill and Hillary Clinton. He was an international partner with the Sawyer-Miller consulting firm and was a senior adviser to FTI Consulting.

Smartmatic has already encountered controversy in the ongoing presidential contest. It ran the online balloting for the Utah Republican caucus last March, when many critics said it was impossible to secure personal electronic devices that are used to register and vote.

Fractionalized votes and GEMS

A report by Bev Harris summarizes her review of the GEMS election management system, which counts approximately 25 percent of all votes in the United States. The results of this study demonstrate that a fractional vote feature is embedded in each GEMS application which can be used to invisibly, yet radically, alter election outcomes by pre-setting desired vote percentages to redistribute votes. This tampering is not visible to election observers, even if they are standing in the room and watching the computer. Use of the decimalized vote feature is unlikely to be detected by auditing or canvass procedures, and can be applied across large jurisdictions in less than 60 seconds.

EMS vote-counting systems are and have been operated under five trade names: Global Election Systems, Diebold Election Systems, Premier Election Systems, Dominion Voting Systems, and Election Systems & Software, in addition to a number of private regional subcontractors. The system is used statewide in nearly 30 states and Canada

Weighting a race removes the principle of "one person-one vote". It allow votes to be counted as less than one or more than one. Regardless of real votes, candidates can receive a set percentage of votes. Results can be preset. For example, Candidate A can be assigned 44% of the votes, Candidate B 51%, and Candidate C the rest.

GEMS fractionalizes votes in three places:

1 "Summary" vote tally of totals for each race on Election Night
2 "Statement of Votes Cast": results by precinct and voting method (polling, absentee, early, provisional).
3 "Undervotes"

Part 1: Votes are counted as fractions instead of Integers
http://blackboxvoting.org/fraction-magic-1

Part 2: Context, Background, Deeper, Worse
http://blackboxvoting.org/fraction-magic-2

Part 3: Proof of code
http://blackboxvoting.org/fraction-magic-3

Part 4: Presidential race in an entire state switched in four seconds
http://blackboxvoting.org/fraction-magic-4

Part 5: Masters of the Universe
http://blackboxvoting.org/fraction-magic-5

Part 6: Execution capacity – coming –
 http://blackboxvoting.org/fraction-magic-6
Part 7: Solutions and Mitigations – coming –
 http://blackboxvoting.org/fraction-magic-7

Illegal voters

In the United States, there are over 3.5 million more people registered to vote than there are living adult citizens.

Under federal law, the 1993 National Voter Registration Act and the 2002 Help America Vote Act REQUIRE states to maintain accurate voter lists. Nonetheless, some state politicians ignore this law. Governor Terry McAuliffe, D-Virginia, vetoed a measure mandating investigations of elections in which ballots outnumbered eligible voters.

The Election Integrity Project of **Judicial Watch**, a Washington-based legal-watchdog group, analyzed data from the U.S. Census Bureau's 2011 - 2015 American Community Survey and last month's statistics from the federal Election Assistance Commission. The latter included figures from 38 states. According to Judicial Watch, 11 states gave the EAC insufficient or questionable information. Pennsylvania's legitimate numbers place it just below the over-registration threshold.

Judicial Watch's state-by-state results yielded 462 counties where the registration rate exceeded 100 percent. There were 3,551,760 more people registered to vote than adult U.S. citizens who inhabit these counties.

Among some 2,500 U.S. counties for which Judicial Watch had data, 462 (18.5 percent) exhibit this ghost-voter problem. Washington's Clark County has a 154 percent over-registration rate, including 166,811 ghost voters. Georgia's Fulton County is 108 percent over-registration.

California's San Diego County is 138 percent over-registration (810,966 ghost voters). Los Angeles County's 112 percent rate equals 707,475 over-registrations. Judicial Watch reports that L.A. County employees "informed us that the total number of registered voters now stands at a number that is a whopping 144 percent of the total number of resident citizens of voting age." (1,736,556 ghost voters).

Judicial Watch last week wrote Democratic Secretary of State Alex Padilla and authorities in 11 counties and documented how their election records are in shambles. "California's voting rolls are an absolute mess that undermines the very idea of clean elections," said Judicial Watch President Tom Fitton. "It is urgent that California take reasonable steps to clean up its rolls. We will sue if state officials fail to act."

In the battleground states, Electoral College votes can be decided by narrow margins. Consider ghost voters in: Colorado: 159,373, Florida: 100,782, Iowa: 31,077, Michigan: 225,235, New Hampshire: 8,211, North Carolina: 189,721, Virginia: 89,979

Noncitizens and illegal aliens are counted when apportioning congressional districts and when allocating state electors under the Electoral College. Mass immigration has had a significant effect on American electoral politics. Despite the fact that it is a crime for aliens to vote in federal elections, noncitizens and illegal aliens are counted when apportioning congressional districts.

The National Voter Registration Act of 1993 (NVRA) requires that persons registering to vote in federal elections affirm that they are United States Citizens. Failure to do so is a crime punishable under the following statutes

The preferred form of documentary identification in the United States is the drivers' license. Currently, twelve states and the District of Columbia allow illegal aliens to obtain a drivers' license.[10]

The information supplied by license applicants doubles as voter registration information and the registration process has become nearly automatic. It is relatively easy for aliens to commit voter fraud through the Motor-Voter system. When renewing a driver's license by mail, they simply check the boxes indicating that they wish to be registered as voters and affirming that they are a U.S. citizen. Most often, they are added to the voter rolls without any attempt to verify the applicant's citizenship.

Estimates of the illegal population vary between 11 and 20 million. FAIR believes there are likely between 11 to 13 million illegal residents. The Census Bureau estimates that the illegal alien population is growing by a minimum of 500,000 per year.

Combining the estimated numbers of both legal and illegal aliens, there appear to be at least 22 million non-U.S. citizens in the United States (lawful permanent residents and illegal aliens).

In a 2013 National Hispanic Survey by pollster John McLaughlin, 13% of 800 likely Hispanic voters admitted they were not American citizens.

In 2014, a study released by a team of professors from Old Dominion University and George Mason University estimated that approximately 6.4 percent of noncitizens voted In the 2008 presidential election. They also surmised that 2.2 percent voted in the 2010 midterm election.

 If we take the mean of these three estimates -- 7.25 percent -- and apply it to the 22 million non-citizen residents currently in the United States, then approximately 1.6 million non-citizens vote every year. That number could be as high as 2.9 million (at 13 percent of 22 million), or as low as 528,000 (2.4 percent of 22 million).

Illegal votes may in part explain why Hillary won the popular vote. A Rasmussen Reports poll earlier this year found that 53% of the Democratic Party supports letting illegals vote, even though it's against the law. Hillary said in the debates that it was "horrifying" if a defeated candidate wouldn't recognize the results of the election

When Donald Trump tweeted: "In addition to winning the Electoral College in a landslide, I won the popular vote if you deduct the millions of people who voted illegally,"

The Nation declared: "The President-Elect Is an Internet Troll." Washington Post's "The Fix" blog site: "Donald Trump's new explanation for losing the popular vote? A Twitter-born conspiracy theory."

The media taking point was that Trump was influenced by the faulty analysis of Gregg Phillips of True The Vote who estimated that illegals cast three million votes in the 2016 election.

Some states, including California, Virginia and New York, have political movements to legalize voting by noncitizens. The Census estimates that at least 11 million to 12 million illegals in the U.S.

In a 2014 study in the online Electoral Studies Journal, the authors say that illegals may have cast as many as 2.8 million votes in 2008 and 2010. Considering that the population of illegals has increased since then, so must have their vote.

Critics note that a Harvard team in 2015 had responded to the study, calling it "biased." The report stated: "Further, the likely percent of noncitizen voters in recent U.S. elections is 0." That's simply ridiculous. Just look at California. Leftist get-out-the-vote groups openly urge noncitizens to vote, and the registration process is notoriously loose.

When the far left began insinuating that the Russians had hacked the election, the media treated the unsupported claims with the utmost of respect. But they lambasted Trump for saying that illegals voted mainly for Democratic candidates, including Hillary Clinton.

Voter Registration Lists

Judicial Watch sent a notice-of-violation letter to the state of California and 11 of its counties threatening to sue in federal court if it does not clean its voter registration lists as mandated by the National Voter Registration Act (NVRA). Both the NVRA and the federal Help America Vote Act require states to take reasonable steps to maintain accurate voting rolls. The August 1 letter was sent on behalf of several Judicial Watch California supporters and the Election Integrity Project California, Inc.

Judicial Watch noted that public records obtained on the Election Assistance Commission's 2016 Election Administration Voting Survey and through verbal accounts from various county agencies show 11 California counties have more registered voters than voting-age citizens: Imperial (102%), Lassen (102%), Los Angeles (112%), Monterey (104%), San Diego (138%), San Francisco (114%), San Mateo (111%), Santa Cruz (109%), Solano (111%), Stanislaus (102%), and Yolo (110%).

It also noted that Los Angeles County officials "informed us that the total number of registered voters now stands at a number that is a whopping 144% of the total number of resident citizens of voting age."

"California's voting rolls are an absolute mess that undermines the very idea of clean elections," Judicial Watch President Tom Fitton said. "It is urgent that California take reasonable steps to clean up its rolls. We will sue if state officials fail to act."

In April, Judicial Watch sent notice-of-violation letters threatening to sue 11 states having counties in which the number of registered voters exceeds the number of voting-age citizens: Alabama, Florida, Georgia, Illinois, Iowa, Kentucky, Maryland, New Jersey, New York, North Carolina and Tennessee.

On July 18, Judicial Watch filed a lawsuit against Montgomery County and the Maryland State Boards of Elections under the NVRA. The lawsuit was filed in the U.S. District Court for the District of Maryland, Baltimore Division (JUDICIAL WATCH VS. LINDA H. LAMONE, ET AL. (No. 1:17-cv-02006)).

Election Integrity Project California, Inc. is a registered non-profit corporation that seeks to preserve a government of, by, and for the people. To that end, Election Integrity Project California empowers citizen volunteers through education and training to protect the integrity of the electoral process in California.

The director of Judicial Watch's Election Integrity Project is senior attorney Robert Popper, who was formerly deputy chief of the Voting Section of the Civil Rights Division of the Justice Department.

Crosscheck

According to election investigator Greg Palast, the 2016 election is the culmination of a decade-long Republican effort to disenfranchise voters under the guise of battling voter fraud.

"Election officials in more than two dozen states have compiled lists of citizens whom they allege could be registered in more than one state – thus potentially able to cast multiple ballots – and eligible to be purged from the voter rolls.

The data is processed through the Interstate Voter Registration Crosscheck Program, which is being promoted by a powerful Republican operative Kansas Secretary of State Kris Kobach, a Yale-educated former law professor. Its lists of potential duplicate voters are kept confidential. But *Rolling Stone* obtained a portion of the list and the names of 1 million targeted voters. The Crosscheck list disproportionately threatens solid Democratic constituencies: young, black, Hispanic and Asian-American voters. The biggest possible purges underway in Ohio and North Carolina, two crucial swing states with tight Senate races.

Twenty-eight participating states share their voter lists. To make sure the system finds suspect voters, Crosscheck supposedly matches first, middle and last name, plus birth date, and provides the last four digits of a Social Security number for additional verification. In reality, however, there have been signs that the program doesn't operate as advertised. Some states have dropped out of Crosscheck, citing problems with its methodology, as Oregon's secretary of state recently explained: "We left [Crosscheck] because the data we received was unreliable."

Palast contacted every state for their Crosscheck list. But because voting twice is a felony, state after state told us their lists of suspects were part of a criminal investigation and, as such, confidential. Then we got a break. A clerk in Virginia sent us its Crosscheck list of suspects, which a letter from the state later said was done "in error."

In all, 342,556 names were listed as apparently registered to vote in both Virginia and another state as of January 2014. Thirteen percent of the people on the Crosscheck list, already flagged as inactive voters, were almost immediately removed, meaning 41,637 names were cancelled from voter rolls, most of them just before Election Day.

If Virginia's 13 percent is any indication, almost 1 million Americans will have their right to vote challenged. Analysis suggests that winding up on the Crosscheck list is hardly proof that an individual is registered in more than one state. Almost all Crosscheck states are Republican-controlled".

Voter Suppression

Donald Trump clinched the presidency by securing victories in two critical swing states: Wisconsin and North Carolina. In Wisconsin, Trump won by about 3 percentage points; in North Carolina, 4. It is, of course, impossible to know what factors contributed to Trump's victories in these states.

In Wisconsin, the Republican-dominated Legislature passed a series of "reforms" designed to suppress the votes of minorities and college students. The Legislature slashed early voting, especially in minority communities, and passed draconian new voter ID requirements that effectively disenfranchised many underprivileged black voters. One federal judge found that the Legislature had explicitly targeted certain black people on the basis of race and attempted to suppress their votes. But an appeals court pushed back against several district court rulings softening the law, leaving much of it in place for the 2016 election. As a result, many people were unable to obtain necessary identification documents and cast ballots in Wisconsin this year.

North Carolina's election laws are exempt from federal oversight. The Legislature passed a bill seriously curtailing voting rights. The U.S. Court of Appeals for the 4th Circuit stated that the bill "targeted African Americans with almost surgical precision," slashing early voting on days that blacks disproportionately favored.

The court blocked the legislation from taking effect. Republican-controlled county election boards implemented the early voting cuts anyway. The state also dramatically reduced the number of polling places throughout the state.

As a result, more voters had less time to cast ballots and were forced to wait in longer lines at less convenient locations. Most voters inconvenienced by these changes were minorities—as were a majority of voters illegally purged from the rolls by Republican activists in the months before the election. Some, but not all, of these purged voters' rights were restored in time for Election Day.

APPENDIX

A. Nine Pre-election Polls

9 Polls Gallup	Clinton	Trump	Johnson	Stein
Ind 40.0%	33.8%	43.6%	8.9%	3.8%
Dem 32.0%	88.1%	6.9%	1.3%	1.7%
Rep 28.0%	5.6%	87.8%	3.9%	0.3%
Pre-UVA 94.7%	**43.3%**	**44.2%**	**5.1%**	**2.1%**
Votes 128,963	**55,792**	**57,007**	**6,540**	**2,757**
EVote 538	**232**	**306**		
Adjusted	**44.4%**	**47.6%**	**5.1%**	**2.1%**
Votes 136,216	**60,471**	**64,836**	**6,908**	**2,912**
Evote 538	**182**	**356**		

9 Polls NEP	Clinton	Trump	Johnson	Stein
Ind 31.0%	33.8%	43.6%	8.9%	3.8%
Dem 36.0%	88.1%	6.9%	1.3%	1.7%
Rep 33.0%	5.6%	87.8%	3.9%	0.3%
Pre-UVA 95.3%	**44.0%**	**44.9%**	**4.5%**	**1.9%**
Votes 129,914	**57,194**	**58,395**	**5,871**	**2,444**
EVote 538	**212**	**326**		
Adjusted	**45.0%**	**47.8%**	**4.5%**	**1.9%**
Votes 136,216	**61,271**	**65,137**	**6,155**	**2,562**
Evote 538	**216**	**327**		

NEP	NEP	Clinton	Trump	Johnson	Stein
Ind	28.9%	42.0%	46.0%	5.0%	5.0%
Dem	38.7%	89.0%	8.0%	0.0%	3.0%
Rep	29.3%	8.0%	88.0%	4.0%	0.0%
Pre-UVA	96.9%	48.9%	42.2%	2.6%	2.6%
Votes	131,978	64,529	55,689	3,455	3,437
Evote	538	418	120		
Adjusted		49.7%	44.5%	2.6%	2.6%
Votes	136,216	67,660	60,655	3,566	3,548
Evote	538	369	169		

NEP	Gallup	Clinton	Trump	Johnson	Stein
Ind	38.0%	42.0%	46.0%	5.0%	5.0%
Dem	30.5%	89.0%	8.0%	0.0%	3.0%
Rep	27.0%	8.0%	88.0%	4.0%	0.0%
Pre-UVA	95.5%	45.3%	43.7%	3.0%	2.8%
Votes	130,513	59,077	57,008	3,889	3,674
Evote	538	281	257		
Adjusted		46.4%	47.1%	3.0%	0.76%
Votes	136,216	63,191	64,096	4,059	3,834
Evote		250	288		

Polls	Prty-ID Ind	Dem	Rep	Poll Clinton	Trump	Vote Clinton	Trump	75% Undec	Reported Clinton	Trump
Ipsos	17%	45%	32%	42.0%	39.0%	298	240	10.0%	44.5%	46.5%
IBD	37%	34%	29%	43.0%	45.0%	202	336	2.0%	43.5%	46.5%
Rasmussen	32%	40%	27%	45.0%	43.0%	313	225	6.0%	46.5%	47.5%
Quinnipiac	26%	40%	34%	47.0%	40.0%	378	160	5.0%	48.3%	43.8%
Fox News	25%	43%	29%	48.0%	44.0%	317	221	1.0%	48.3%	44.8%
CNN	43%	31%	26%	49.0%	44.0%	362	176	2.0%	49.5%	45.5%
ABC	29%	37%	30%	47.0%	44.0%	317	221	3.0%	47.8%	46.3%
Gravis	27%	40%	33%	47.0%	45.0%	294	244	4.0%	48.0%	48.0%
LA Times	30%	38%	32%	44.0%	47.0%	202	336	0.0%	44.0%	47.0%
Average	29.6%	38.7%	30.2%	45.8%	43.4%	298.1	239.9	5.4%	46.7%	46.2%

Gallup	Ind %			Gallup		EV		75%	Post UVA	
Ipsos	21%	33%	12%	36.0%	36.8%	239	299	14.1%	39.5%	47.4%
IBD	30%	47%	17%	41.9%	45.3%	202	336	2.0%	42.4%	46.9%
Rasmussen	30%	42%	12%	40.6%	45.3%	167	371	7.0%	42.4%	50.6%
Quinnipiac	37%	42%	5%	44.7%	40.8%	335	203	5.9%	46.2%	45.2%
Fox News	39%	44%	5%	45.8%	43.9%	298	240	1.4%	46.1%	44.9%
CNN	43%	44%	1%	48.6%	44.4%	335	203	2.0%	49.2%	46.0%
ABC	40%	49%	9%	46.8%	47.0%	249	289	0.6%	46.9%	47.5%
Gravis	32%	43%	11%	43.6%	45.5%	216	322	8.0%	45.6%	51.5%
LA Times	32%	52%	20%	41.7%	48.2%	85	453	2.0%	42.2%	49.7%
Average	33.8%	44.0%	10.2%	43.3%	44.1%	236.2	301.8	4.8%	44.2%	48.5%
Elec Vote						232	306		Wtd 180	358
Expected					224		314		EV 172.6	365.4

REPORTED		Prty-ID			Poll		Electoral Vote	
POLLS	Ind	Dem	Rep		Clinton	Trump	Clinton	Trump
1 Reuters	16%	45%	38%		42.0%	39.0%	298	240
2 IBD	37%	34%	29%		43.0%	45.0%	202	336
3 Rasmussen	32%	40%	28%		45.0%	43.0%	313	225
4 Quinnipiac	26%	40%	34%		47.0%	40.0%	378	160
5 Fox News	19%	43%	38%		48.0%	44.0%	317	221
6 CNN	43%	31%	26%		49.0%	44.0%	362	176
7 ABC	29%	37%	29%		47.0%	43.0%	317	221
8 Gravis	27%	40%	33%		47.0%	45.0%	294	244
9 LA Times	30%	38%	32%		44.0%	47.0%	202	336
Average	**28.8%**	**38.7%**	**31.9%**		**45.8%**	**43.3%**	**298**	**240**

ADJUSTED		Ind%			Poll (Gallup)		Electoral Vote	
40I-32D-28R	Clinton	Trump	Diff		Clinton	Trump	Clinton	Trump
1 Reuters	21%	29%	8%		36.0%	36.8%	239	299
2 IBD	30%	47%	17%		41.9%	45.3%	202	336
3 Rasmussen	30%	42%	12%		40.6%	45.3%	167	371
4 Quinnipiac	37%	42%	5%		44.7%	40.8%	335	203
5 Fox News	39%	44%	5%		45.8%	43.9%	298	240
6 CNN	43%	44%	1%		48.6%	44.4%	335	203
7 ABC	40%	49%	9%		46.8%	47.0%	249	289
8 Gravis	32%	43%	11%		43.6%	45.5%	216	322
9 LA Times	32%	52%	20%		41.7%	48.2%	85	453
Average	**33.8%**	**43.6%**	**9.8%**		**42.9%**	**44.4%**	**236**	**302**
EV							**232**	**306**

B. True Vote Model –Returning Voters

According to the adjusted 1972, 1988, 1992, 2004 and 2008 National Exit Polls, there were millions more returning Nixon, Bush 1 and Bush 2 voters from the previous election than were still living – a mathematical impossibility and proof of election fraud.

It's obvious that there must be fewer returning voters than the number who voted in the prior election. Approximately 5% of voters pass in the four years between elections. ALL exit polls are adjusted (forced) to match the recorded vote. It's no secret. It's the standard, stated policy of the National Election Pool. The insane rationale for the forced match is that the recorded vote is always fraud-free. But the real reason is to hide the extent of fraudulent vote miscounting.

The adjusted, published exit poll is a **Matrix of Deceit.** The True Vote Model (TVM) replaces the impossible, forced adjustments made to the unadjusted exit polls with a feasible, plausible estimate of returning voters.

The TVM applies to all elections Presidential elections are used in this analysis as they are well-known; historical data is readily available. The TVM has been used to analyze congressional, senate and recall elections and has uncovered strong evidence of fraud.

A matrix is a rectangular array of numbers. The **1968-2012 National True Vote Model (TVM)** is an application based on Matrix Algebra. The key to understanding the theory is mathematical subscript notation. The actual mathematics is simple arithmetic.

The model is easy to use. Just two inputs are required: the election year and calculation method (1-5). Calculation methods are the following:

1- National Exit Poll (returning voters (and vote shares) adjusted to match the fraudulent recorded vote)

 Returning voters based on the previous election
2- recorded vote
3- votes cast (including allocated uncounted votes)
4- unadjusted national exit poll
5- True Vote

The **National True Vote Model** is based on total votes cast in the previous and current election. The True Vote Model (TVM) calculates each candidate's share of a) previous election returning voters and b) new voters who did not vote in the previous election. National Exit Poll vote shares were used to calculate the True Vote in each election- except for 2004.

At 12:22am, 13047 exit poll respondents indicated that Kerry was a 51-48% winner. The final 613 respondents (13660) and the returning 2000 voter mix were both adjusted in order to match the recorded vote (Bush 51-48%). Both sets of adjustments were impossible. It was only years later that the complete 2004 unadjusted exit poll was released. It showed that Kerry won the
13660 respondents by 51-47.5%.

The US Vote Census provides an estimate of the number of
votes cast in each election. Total votes cast include uncounted
ballots, as opposed to the official recorded vote. There were
approximately 40 million uncounted votes in the 6 elections from
1988-2008. Uncounted ballots are strongly Democratic.

The **1988-2012 State True Vote Model** is based on returning state voters. The Governor, senate and congressional True Vote models work the same way.

Sensitivity Matrix: The tables gauge the sensitivity of the total candidate vote shares to changes in their shares of returning and new voters.

In 2004 Bush won the recorded vote by 3 million (50.7-48.3%). However, at the 12:22am National Exit Poll timeline (13047 respondents), Kerry had 91% of returning Gore voters, 10% of returning Bush voters and 57% of New voters. In this base case scenario, Kerry had a 53.6% True Vote share and 10.7 million vote margin. Sensitivity analysis indicates that Kerry won all plausible (and implausible) scenarios. Bush needed an impossible 110% turnout of Bush 2000 voters to win the fraudulent recorded vote.

Adjusting the base case vote shares to view worst case scenarios: 1) Kerry has 91% of returning Gore voters, 8% of returning Bush voters and 53% of New voters. Kerry's vote share is reduced to 52.1% and a 7.2 million winning margin.

2) Kerry has just 89% of returning Gore voters, 8% of returning Bush voters and 57% of new voters. Kerry's total vote share is reduced to 52.0% and a 6.9 million margin.

3) Assume the base case vote shares, change the returning 2000 voter turnout rate to 94% for Gore and 100% for Bush. Kerry's share is reduced to 52.7% (8.5 million).

4) Assume 98% turnout of returning Gore and Bush voters. Kerry had 91% of returning Gore voters. To match the recorded vote, Bush needed 61% of new voters; he had a 41% exit poll share. He needed 96% of returning Bush voters; he had a 90% exit poll share. The required shares easily exceeded the 2% margin of error.

In 2004, 125.7 million votes were cast. New voters (TVN) is the difference between 2004 votes cast (TVC) and returning 2000 voters (RV): TVN = TVC – RV; TVN = 24.5 = 125.7 – 103.2

In the True Vote Model, returning voters (RV) from the prior election are estimated based on voter mortality (5%) and estimated turnout (TR).

Let TVP = total votes cast the in previous election.
Let TVC = total votes cast in the current election.
V (1) = returning Democratic voters
V (2) = returning Republican voters
V (3) = returning other (third-party) voters
RV = V (1) + V (2) + V (3) = total returning voters
V (4) = TVC – RV = number of new voters.

Let a (i, j) =candidate (j) vote shares of returning and new voters
m (i) = V (i) / TVC, i=1, 4 (m (i) is the percentage mix of total votes cast for returning and new voters)

Democratic share:
$VS(1) = \sum m(i) * a(i, 1)$, i=1,4
VS(1)= m(1)*a(1,1) + m(2)*a(2,1) + m(3)*a(3,1) + m(4)*a(4,1)
Republican share:
VS(2)= m(2)*a(1,2) + m(2)*a(2,2) + m(3)*a(3,2) + m(4)*a(4,2)
Third-party share:
VS(3)= m(3)*a(1,3) + m(2)*a(2,3) + m(3)*a(3,3) + m(4)*a(4,3)

Total candidate shares of returning and new voters.
$\sum m (i) = 100\%$, i= 1, 4

Candidate shares of returning and new voters.
$\sum a (1, j) = 100\%$, j=1, 3
$\sum a (2, j) = 100\%$, j=1, 3
$\sum a (3, j) = 100\%$, j=1, 3
$\sum a (4, j) = 100\%$, j=1, 3

Democratic + Republican + third-party vote shares.
$\sum VS (i) = 100\%$, i=1,3

C. State Exit Polls and True Vote Models

Battleground States: Gallup Party-ID

Pct	Clinton	Trump	Johnson	Stein
Ind 40%	40%	48%	8%	4%
Dem 32%	89%	5%	2%	4%
Rep 28%	5%	90%	4%	1%
Calc	**45.9%**	**46.0%**	**5.0%**	**3.2%**
Poll	**45.4%**	**42.9%**	**5.4%**	**1.3%**
Diff	**0.5%**	**3.1%**	**-0.4%**	**1.9%**
BG	**45.1%**	**46.9%**	**4.9%**	**3.1%**

	Clinton	Trump	Johnson	Stein	Trump EV	Clinton
AZ	41.6%	49.7%	5.5%	3.2%	11	
CO	42.8%	48.6%	5.5%	3.2%	9	
FL	45.2%	46.5%	5.0%	3.2%	29	
GA	43.1%	49.1%	4.8%	3.0%	16	
IA	43.1%	48.1%	5.5%	3.2%	6	
ME	44.8%	46.2%	5.6%	3.4%	4	
MI	46.7%	45.4%	4.7%	3.1%		16
MN	46.2%	46.1%	4.7%	3.1%		10
MO	42.8%	49.5%	4.8%	3.0%	10	
NC	47.7%	44.0%	5.1%	3.3%		15
NV	45.7%	46.1%	5.0%	3.2%	6	
OH	44.2%	48.1%	4.7%	3.0%	18	
PA	49.0%	43.5%	4.5%	3.1%		20
VA	43.8%	48.4%	4.8%	3.0%	13	

		Unadj Exit Poll		Trump	Reported		Trump
	Votes	Clinton	Trump	EV	Clinton	Trump	EV
AZ	2,573	46.8%	48.2%	11	45.1%	48.7%	11
CO	2,780	46.5%	41.5%		48.2%	43.3%	
FL	9,420	47.7%	46.4%		47.8%	49.0%	29
GA	4,115	46.8%	48.2%	16	45.6%	50.8%	16
IA	1,566	44.1%	48.0%	6	41.7%	51.1%	6
ME	748	51.2%	40.2%		47.8%	44.9%	4
MI	4,799	46.8%	46.8%	16	47.3%	47.5%	16
MN	2,945	45.7%	45.8%	10	46.4%	44.9%	
MO	2,809	42.8%	51.2%	10	38.1%	56.8%	10
NC	4,742	48.6%	46.5%		46.2%	49.8%	15
NV	1,125	48.7%	42.8%		47.9%	45.5%	
OH	5,496	47.0%	47.1%	18	43.6%	51.7%	18
PA	5,950	50.5%	46.1%		47.9%	48.6%	20
VA	3,983	50.9%	43.2%		49.8%	44.4%	
WI	2,976	48.2%	44.3%		46.5%	47.2%	10
Unwtd	56,027	47.5%	45.8%	87	46.0%	48.3%	155
Wtd		47.6%	46.2%		46.3%	48.7%	
28 Exit Poll							
411	110,702	49.6%	43.6%	159	49.3%	45.2%	224

Average State Exit Poll Party-ID vs Gallup

	Pct	Clinton	Trump	Other	Gallup	Clinton	Trump	Other
Dem	38.7%	88.4%	6.0%	3.0%	32%	88.4%	6.0%	3.0%
Rep	29.3%	5.0%	87.8%	4.0%	28%	5.0%	87.8%	4.0%
Ind	28.9%	33.9%	42.7%	13.0%	40%	33.8%	42.7%	13.0%
Total	100.0%	47.4%	46.2%	6.4%	100%	44.6%	47.7%	7.3%
Votes	136.22	64.59	62.95	8.68	136.22	60.71	64.93	9.92
		Margin	-1.64	-1.20%		Margin	4.22	

National Exit Poll vs Gallup

	Pct	Clinton	Trump	Other	Gallup	Clinton	Trump	Other
Dem	36%	89%	8%	3%	32%	87%	9%	4%
Rep	33%	8%	88%	4%	28%	6%	91%	3%
Ind	31%	42%	46%	12%	40%	40%	48%	12%
Total	100%	47.7%	46.2%	6.1%	100%	45.5%	47.6%	6.9%
		Margin	-2.07	-1.5%		Margin	2.78	2.0%

Gender	Pct	Clinton	Trump	Other	Pct	Clinton	Trump	Other
male	47%	41%	53%	6%	47%	38%	56%	6%
female	53%	54%	42%	4%	53%	51%	41%	8%
Total	100%	47.9%	47.2%	4.9%	100%	44.9%	48.0%	7.1%
		-0.98	-0.72%			4.30	3.1%	

23 states –no EP

Reported	EV	Votes	Clinton	Trump	Clinton	Trump
Total	**127**	**25,350**	**43.7%**	**50.4%**	**11,079**	**12,777**
TN	11	2,508	34.7%	60.7%	871	1,523
AL	9	2,123	34.4%	62.1%	730	1,318
OK	7	1,453	28.9%	65.3%	420	949
LA	8	2,029	38.4%	58.1%	780	1,179
AR	6	1,131	33.7%	60.6%	380	685
WV	5	713	26.5%	68.6%	189	489
KS	6	1,184	36.1%	56.7%	427	671
ID	4	690	27.5%	59.3%	190	409
MS	6	1,209	40.1%	57.9%	485	701
NE	5	844	33.7%	58.7%	284	496
ND	3	344	27.2%	63.0%	94	217
WY	3	256	21.9%	68.2%	56	174
SD	3	370	31.7%	61.5%	117	228
MT	3	497	35.7%	56.2%	178	279
AK	3	319	36.6%	51.3%	116	163
DE	3	442	53.4%	41.9%	236	185
RI	4	414	54.8%	40.2%	227	166
VT	3	320	55.7%	29.8%	179	95
HI	4	438	61.0%	29.4%	267	129
CT	7	1,645	54.6%	40.9%	898	673
DC	3	313	90.5%	4.1%	283	13
MD	10	2,781	60.3%	33.9%	1,678	943
MA	11	3,325	60.0%	32.8%	1,995	1,091

28 Exit Poll states

Party-ID	Votes	Exit Poll Dem	Rep	Ind	Gallup Dem	Rep	Ind
National	110.70	36	33	31	31.0	28.0	41.0
Wtd Avg		37.46	31.76	30.78	32.3	26.9	40.8
AZ	2,573	28.0	32.0	40.0	24.1	27.2	48.7
CA	14,182	47.0	23.0	30.0	40.5	19.5	40.0
CO	2,780	32.0	24.0	44.0	27.6	20.4	52.1
FL	9,420	32.0	33.0	35.0	27.6	28.0	44.4
GA	4,115	34.0	36.0	30.0	29.3	30.5	40.2
IA	1,566	31.0	34.0	35.0	26.7	28.8	44.5
IL	5,536	45.0	30.0	25.0	38.8	25.5	35.8
IN	2,741	34.0	39.0	27.0	29.3	33.1	37.6
KY	1,924	38.0	44.0	18.0	32.7	37.3	29.9
ME	748	32.0	27.0	41.0	27.6	22.9	49.5
MI	4,799	40.0	31.0	29.0	34.4	26.3	39.3
MN	2,945	37.0	35.0	28.0	31.9	29.7	38.4
MO	2,809	34.0	39.0	27.0	29.3	33.1	37.6
NC	4,742	35.0	31.0	34.0	30.1	26.3	43.6
NH	742	28.0	28.0	44.0	24.1	23.8	52.1
NJ	3,907	43.0	27.0	30.0	37.0	22.9	40.1
NM	798	41.0	27.0	32.0	35.3	22.9	41.8
NV	1,125	36.0	28.0	36.0	31.0	23.8	45.2
NY	7,456	48.0	26.0	26.0	41.3	22.1	36.6
OH	5,496	34.0	37.0	29.0	29.3	31.4	39.3
PA	5,950	41.0	39.0	20.0	35.3	33.1	31.6
SC	2,103	27.0	46.0	27.0	23.3	39.0	37.7
TX	8,969	29.0	38.0	33.0	25.0	32.2	42.8

Party-ID	Votes	Exit Poll Dem	Rep	Ind	Gallup Dem	Rep	Ind
UT	1,131	20.0	45.0	35.0	17.2	38.2	44.6
VA	3,983	40.0	33.0	27.0	34.4	28.0	37.6
WA	3,184	34.0	20.0	46.0	29.3	17.0	53.8
WI	2,976	35.0	35.0	30.0	30.1	29.7	40.2

Total 51 states

	Clinton	Trump	Johnson	Stein
28 EP states	45.77%	47.67%	6.56%	1.91%
Votes	50,664	52,776	7,261	2,112
23 states	43.71%	50.40%	5.89%	6.70%
Voted	11,079	12,777	1,493	1,698
51 states	**45.33%**	**48.13%**	**6.54%**	**2.80%**
Votes	**61,744**	**65,554**	**8,754**	**3,810**

Ohio True Vote Model- Party-ID

Exit Poll	Pct	Clinton	Trump	Johnson	Stein
Dem	34%	87%	12%	0%	1%
Rep	37%	8%	89%	2%	1%
Ind	**29%**	**50%**	**35%**	**8%**	**7%**
Match	100%	47.0%	47.2%	3.1%	2.7%
Unadj EP	**100%**	**47.0%**	**47.1%**	**3.2%**	**2.7%**
Votes	5,496	2,583	2,589	176	148
		Margin	5	0.1%	

Recorded	Pct	Clinton	Trump	Johnson	Stein
Dem	34%	87%	12%	0%	1%
Rep	37%	8%	89%	2%	1%
Ind	**29%**	**38%**	**51%**	**8%**	**3%**
Match	100%	43.6%	51.8%	3.1%	1.6%
Recorded	**99.3%**	**43.6%**	**51.7%**	**3.2%**	**0.8%**
Votes	5,496	2,394	2,841	174	46
		Margin	447	8.1%	

True Vote	Gallup	Clinton	Trump	Johnson	Stein
Dem	32.4%	87%	12%	0%	1%
Rep	33.4%	8%	89%	2%	1%
Ind	**34.2%**	**38%**	**51%**	**8%**	**3%**
Match	100.0%	43.9%	51.1%	3.4%	1.7%
TVM	**100%**	**43.1%**	**50.2%**	**4.0%**	**2.7%**
Votes	5,496	2,368	2,760	220	149
		Margin	392	4.9%	

Ohio True Vote Model- Returning 2012 Voters

Recorded

2012	Pct	Clinton	Trump	Other	
Obama	46.9%	82.0%	14.0%	4.0%	
Romney	44.2%	5.0%	93.0%	2.0%	
Other	1.5%	20.0%	20.0%	60.0%	
DNV (new)	7.4%	35.0%	51.0%	14.0%	Margin
	Recorded	43.6%	51.7%	4.7%	8.1%
Votes	5,496,487	2,395,126	2,842,537	258,824	447,412

True Vote

2012	Pct	Clinton	Trump	Other	
Obama	44.0%	82.0%	14.0%	4.0%	
Romney	44.2%	5.0%	93.0%	2.0%	
Other	1.5%	20.0%	20.0%	60.0%	
DNV (new)	10.4%	35.0%	51.0%	14.0%	Margin
	True Vote	42.2%	52.8%	5.0%	10.6%
Votes	5,496,487	2,318,574	2,902,802	275,111	584,227

North Carolina True Vote Model- Party-ID

Exit Poll	Pct	Clinton	Trump	Johnson	Stein
Dem	35%	90%	8%	1%	1%
Rep	31%	4%	94%	2%	0%
Ind	34%	47%	43%	8%	2%
Match	100%	48.7%	46.6%	3.7%	1.0%
Unadj EP	100%	48.6%	46.5%	4.0%	0.9%
Votes	4,742	2,304	2,205	190	43
		Margin	-100	-2.1%	

Recorded	Pct	Clinton	Trump	Johnson	Stein
Dem	35%	90%	8%	1%	1%
Rep	31%	4%	94%	2%	0%
Ind	34%	39%	53%	8%	0%
Match	100%	46.0%	50.0%	3.7%	0.4%
Recorded	99.0%	46.2%	49.8%	2.7%	0.3%
Votes	4,742	2,189	2,363	130	12
		Margin	173	3.7%	

	Pct	Clinton	Trump	Johnson	Stein
Dem	32.9%	90%	8%	1%	1%
Rep	24.2%	4%	94%	2%	0%
Ind	42.9%	39%	53%	8%	0%
Match	100.0%	47.3%	48.1%	4.2%	0.3%
TVM	100.0%	46.1%	46.4%	4.0%	3.4%
Votes	4,742	2,187	2,202	190	163
		Margin	15	0.8%	

North Carolina True Vote Model- Returning 2012 Voters

Recorded

2012	Pct	Clinton	Trump	Other	
Obama	41.9%	89.0%	7.0%	4.0%	
Romney	43.7%	7.0%	91.0%	2.0%	
Other	1.1%	20.0%	20.0%	60.0%	
DNV (new)	13.3%	42.0%	52.0%	6.0%	Margin
Recorded		46.2%	49.8%	4.0%	3.7%
Votes	4,741,665	2,189,181	2,362,674	189,810	173,493

True Vote

2012	Pct	Clinton	Trump	Other	
Obama	39.3%	89.0%	7.0%	4.0%	
Romney	43.7%	7.0%	91.0%	2.0%	
Other	1.1%	20.0%	20.0%	60.0%	
DNV (new)	16.0%	42.0%	52.0%	6.0%	Margin
True Vote		44.9%	51.0%	4.1%	6.1%
Votes	4,741,665	2,130,208	2,419,138	192,319	288,930

Florida True Vote Model- Party-ID

Exit Poll	Pct	Clinton	Trump	Johnson	Stein	Other
Dem	32%	90%	8%	0%	1%	1%
Rep	33%	8%	89%	1%	1%	1%
Ind	35%	47%	42%	5%	2%	4%
Match	100%	47.9%	46.6%	2.1%	1.4%	2.1%
Unadj EP	100%	47.7%	46.4%	2.0%	1.3%	2.6%
Votes	9,420	4,493	4,371	188	122	245
		Margin	-122	-1.3%		

Recorded	Pct	Clinton	Trump	Johnson	Stein	Other
Dem	32%	90%	8%	0%	1%	1%
Rep	33%	8%	89%	3%	0%	0%
Ind	35%	47%	49%	3%	1%	0%
Match	100%	47.9%	49.1%	2.0%	0.7%	0%
Recorded	100%	47.8%	49.0%	2.2%	0.7%	0.3%
Votes	9,420	4,505	4,618	207	64	26
		Margin	113	1.2%		

TRUE	Gallup	Clinton	Trump	Johnson	Stein	Other
Dem	30.6%	90%	8%	0%	1%	1%
Rep	27.8%	8%	89%	3%	0%	0%
Ind	41.6%	43%	53%	3%	1%	0%
Match	100%	47.7%	49.2%	2.1%	0.7%	0.3%
TVM	100%	44.3%	48.1%	5.1%	2.1%	0.3%
Votes	9,420	4,178	4,532	479	202	28
		Margin	355	3.8%		

Florida True Vote Model- Returning voters

Recorded

2012	Pct	Clinton	Trump	Other	
Obama	41.0%	89.0%	8.0%	3.0%	
Romney	40.3%	7.0%	91.0%	2.0%	
Other	0.7%	20.0%	20.0%	60.0%	
DNV (new)	18.0%	46.5%	49.5%	4.0%	Margin
	Recorded	47.8%	49.0%	3.2%	1.2%
Votes	9,420,039	4,505,395	4,615,161	299,482	109,766

TRUE VOTE

2012	Pct	Clinton	Trump	Other	
Obama	38.4%	89.0%	8.0%	3.0%	
Romney	40.3%	7.0%	91.0%	2.0%	
Other	0.7%	20.0%	20.0%	60.0%	
DNV (new)	20.5%	46.5%	49.5%	4.0%	Margin
	True Vote	46.7%	50.1%	3.2%	3.3%
Votes	9,420,039	4,401,655	4,716,461	301,923	314,806

Wisconsin True Vote Model- Party-ID

Exit Poll	Pct	Clinton	Trump	Johnson	Stein	Other
Dem	35%	91%	7%	1%	1%	0%
Rep	35%	6%	90%	3%	0%	1%
Ind	30%	47%	34%	6%	2%	11%
Match	100%	48.1%	44.2%	3.2%	1.0%	3.7%
Unadjusted	100%	48.2%	44.3%	2.0%	1.3%	4.2%
Votes	2,976	1,435	1,318	60	39	125
		Margin	-116	-3.9%		

Recorded	Pct	Clinton	Trump	Johnson	Stein	Other
Dem	35%	91%	7%	1%	1%	0%
Rep	35%	6%	90%	3%	0%	1%
Ind	30%	43%	46%	6%	2%	3%
Match	100%	46.9%	47.8%	3.2%	1.0%	1.3%
Recorded	100%	46.5%	47.2%	3.6%	1.0%	1.7%
Votes	2,976	1,383	1,405	107	31	51
		Margin	23	0.8%		

TRUE	Gallup	Clinton	Trump	Johnson	Stein	Other
Dem	33.9%	91%	7%	1%	1%	0%
Rep	32.6%	6%	90%	3%	0%	1%
Ind	33.5%	43%	46%	6%	2%	3%
Match	100%	47.2%	47.1%	3.3%	1.0%	1.3%
TVM	100.0%	43.8%	48.2%	4.7%	1.9%	1.3%
Votes	2,976	1,304	1,435	140	58	40
		Margin	132	2.92%		

Wisconsin True Vote Model: Returning voters

Recorded

2012	Pct	Clinton	Trump	Other	
Obama	49.7%	84.0%	10.0%	6.0%	
Romney	43.1%	5.0%	91.0%	4.0%	
Other	1.2%	20.0%	20.0%	60.0%	
DNV (new)	6.0%	40.0%	45.0%	15.0%	Margin
	Recorded	46.5%	47.2%	6.3%	0.6%
Votes	2,976,150	1,384,304	1,403,517	188,329	19,212

TRUE VOTE

2012	Pct	Clinton	Trump	Other	
Obama	46.5%	84.0%	10.0%	6.0%	
Romney	43.1%	5.0%	91.0%	4.0%	
Other	1.2%	20.0%	20.0%	60.0%	
DNV (new)	9.1%	40.0%	45.0%	15.0%	Margin
	True Vote	45.1%	48.3%	6.6%	3.1%
Votes	2,976,150	1,343,222	1,436,196	196,732	92,974

Michigan True Vote Model- Party-ID

Exit Poll	Pct	Clinton	Trump	Johnson	Stein	Other
Dem	40%	88%	9%	2%	1%	0%
Rep	31%	7%	90%	2%	0%	1%
Ind	29%	32%	53%	7%	3%	5%
Match	100%	46.7%	46.9%	3.5%	1.3%	2%
Unadj	100%	46.8%	46.8%	2.3%	1.3%	3%
Votes	4,799	2,246	2,246	110	61	136
		Margin	0	0.0%		

Recorded	Pct	Clinton	Trump	Johnson	Stein	Other
Dem	40%	88%	9%	2%	1%	0%
Rep	31%	7%	90%	2%	0%	1%
Ind	29%	36%	52%	7%	3%	2%
Match	100%	47.8%	46.6%	3.5%	1.3%	0.9%
Recorded	100%	47.3%	47.5%	3.6%	1.1%	0.6%
Votes	4,799	2,269	2,280	172	51	27
		Margin	11	0.2%		

TRUE	Gallup	Clinton	Trump	Johnson	Stein	Other
Dem	34.7%	88%	9%	2%	1%	0%
Rep	29.4%	7%	90%	2%	0%	1%
Ind	35.9%	36%	52%	7%	3%	2%
Match	100%	45.5%	48.3%	3.8%	1.4%	1.0%
TVM	100%	45.2%	46.9%	4.4%	2.4%	1.0%
Votes	4,799	2,172	2,252	213	117	49
		Margin	80	1.7%		

Michigan True Vote Model- Returning voters

Recorded Vote

2012	Pct	Clinton	Trump	Other	
Obama	48.7%	86.0%	11.0%	3.0%	
Romney	40.2%	5.0%	92.0%	3.0%	
Other	1.0%	20.0%	20.0%	60.0%	
DNV (new)	10.1%	32.0%	49.0%	19.0%	Margin
	Recorded	47.3%	47.5%	5.2%	0.1%
Votes	4,799,284	2,272,313	2,278,866	248,105	6,554

TRUE VOTE

2012	Pct	Clinton	Trump	Other	
Obama	45.7%	86.0%	11.0%	3.0%	
Romney	40.2%	5.0%	92.0%	3.0%	
Other	1.0%	20.0%	20.0%	60.0%	
DNV (new)	13.2%	32.0%	49.0%	19.0%	Margin
	True Vote	45.68%	48.65%	5.66%	3.0%
Votes	4,799,284	2,192,545	2,335,000	271,740	142,455

Colorado True Vote Model- Party-ID

Exit Poll	Pct	Clinton	Trump	Johnson	Other
Dem	36%	90%	8%	1%	1%
Rep	28%	8%	88%	2%	2%
Ind	36%	39%	43%	7%	11%
Match	100%	48.7%	43.0%	3.4%	4.9%
Unadjusted	100%	48.7%	42.8%	3.7%	4.8%
Votes	1,125	548	482	42	54
		Margin	-66	-5.9%	
Dem	36%	90%	8%	1%	1%
Rep	28%	8%	88%	2%	2%
Ind	36%	37%	50%	7%	6%
Calc	100%	48.0%	45.5%	3.4%	3.1%
Recorded	100%	47.9%	45.5%	3.3%	3.3%
Votes	1,125	539	512	37	37
		Margin	-27	-2.4%	

TRUE	Gallup	Clinton	Trump	Johnson	Other
Dem	31.3%	90%	8%	1%	1%
Rep	27.5%	8%	88%	2%	2%
Ind	41.2%	37%	50%	6%	7%
TVM1	100.0%	45.6%	47.3%	3.3%	3.7%
TVM	100.0%	43.9%	47.2%	5.1%	3.7%
Votes	1,125	494	531	58	42
		Margin	37	1.7%	

Colorado True Vote Model: Returning Voters

Recorded

2012	Pct	Clinton	Trump	Other	
Obama	43.4%	88.0%	5.0%	7.0%	
Romney	38.9%	8.0%	87.0%	5.0%	
Other	2.0%	20.0%	20.0%	60.0%	
DNV (new)	15.7%	41.5%	44.0%	14.5%	Margin
	Recorded	48.2%	43.3%	8.5%	4.9%
Votes	2,780,220	1,340,782	1,204,111	235,327	136,671

TRUE VOTE

2012	Pct	Clinton	Trump	Other	
Obama	40.7%	88.0%	5.0%	7.0%	
Romney	38.9%	8.0%	87.0%	5.0%	
Other	2.0%	20.0%	20.0%	60.0%	
DNV (new)	18.5%	41.5%	44.0%	14.5%	Margin
	True Vote	47.0%	44.4%	8.7%	2.6%
Votes	2,780,220	1,305,344	1,233,833	241,043	71,511

Virginia True Vote Model- Party-ID

Exit Poll	Pct	Clinton	Trump	Johnson	Stein	Other
Dem	40%	92%	6%	1%	0%	1%
Rep	33%	6%	88%	3%	0%	3%
Ind	27%	47%	45%	6%	2%	0%
Match	100%	51.5%	43.6%	3.0%	0.5%	1%
Unadjusted	100%	50.9%	43.2%	3.7%	0.5%	2%
Votes	3,983	2,027	1,721	147	22	66
		Margin	-307	-7.7%		

Recorded	Pct	Clinton	Trump	Johnson	Stein	Other
Dem	40%	92%	6%	1%	0%	1%
Rep	33%	6%	88%	3%	0%	3%
Ind	27%	43%	48%	6%	2%	1%
Match	100%	50.4%	44.4%	3.0%	0.5%	1.7%
Recorded	100%	49.8%	44.4%	3.0%	0.7%	2.2%
Votes	3,983	1,981	1,769	118	28	86
		Margin	-212	-5.3%		

True		Pct	Clinton	Trump	Johnson	Stein	Other
	Dem	31.3%	90%	8%	1%	1%	
	Rep	27.5%	8%	88%	2%	2%	
	Ind	41.2%	37%	50%	6%	7%	
	Match	100.0%	45.6%	47.3%	3.3%	3.7%	
	TVM	100.0%	43.9%	47.2%	5.1%	3.7%	
	Votes	1,125	494	531	58	42	
			Margin	37	1.7%		

Virginia True Vote Model- Returning voters

Recorded 2012	Pct	Clinton	Trump	Other
Obama	45.2%	92.0%	6.0%	2.0%
Romney	41.7%	8.0%	89.0%	3.0%
Other	1.4%	20.0%	20.0%	60.0%
DNV (new)	11.7%	40.0%	36.0%	24.0%
	Recorded	49.8%	44.4%	5.8%
Votes	3,982,752	1,985,361	1,766,458	230,933

TRUE VOTE

2012	Pct	Clinton	Trump	Other
Obama	42.3%	92.0%	6.0%	2.0%
Romney	41.7%	8.0%	89.0%	3.0%
Other	1.4%	20.0%	20.0%	60.0%
DNV (new)	14.6%	40.0%	36.0%	24.0%
	True Vote	48.4%	45.2%	6.4%
Votes	3,982,752	1,926,301	1,800,531	255,919

Pennsylvania True Vote Model- Party-ID

Exit Poll	Pct	Clinton	Trump	Johnson	Stein
Dem	41%	90%	6%	1%	3%
Rep	39%	8%	91%	1%	0%
Ind	20%	53%	41%	5%	1%
Match	100%	50.6%	46.2%	1.8%	1.4%
Unadjusted	100%	50.5%	46.1%	1.8%	1.6%
Votes	5,950	3,005	2,743	107	95
		Margin	-262	-4.4%	

Reported	Pct	Clinton	Trump	Johnson	Stein
Dem	41%	90%	6%	1%	3%
Rep	39%	8%	91%	1%	0%
Ind	20%	39%	53%	5%	3%
Calc	100%	47.8%	48.6%	1.8%	1.8%
Reported	100%	47.9%	48.6%	2.4%	0.8%
Votes	6,115	2,926	2,971	147	50
		Margin	44	0.7%	

True	Adj	Clinton	Trump	Johnson	Stein
Dem	39.1%	90%	6%	1%	3%
Rep	29.2%	8%	91%	1%	0%
Ind	31.7%	39%	53%	5%	3%
TVM1	100.0%	49.9%	45.7%	2.3%	2.1%
90	95.3%	46.8%	42.1%	4.5%	1.9%
TVM	100.0%	47.9%	45.6%	4.2%	2.3%
Votes	5,950	2,852	2,715	250	135
		Margin	-137	-2.3%	

Pennsylvania True Vote Model- Returning Voters

Recorded Vote

2012	Pct	Clinton	Trump	Other
Obama	44.6%	88.0%	11.0%	1.0%
Romney	40.0%	7.0%	92.0%	1.0%
Other	1.2%	20.0%	20.0%	60.0%
DNV (new)	14.2%	39.5%	47.0%	13.5%
	Recorded	47.9%	48.6%	3.5%
Votes	6,115,402	2,929,007	2,972,094	214,301

TRUE VOTE

2012	Pct	Clinton	Trump	Other
Obama	41.8%	88.0%	11.0%	1.0%
Romney	40.0%	7.0%	92.0%	1.0%
Other	1.2%	20.0%	20.0%	60.0%
DNV (new)	17.0%	39.5%	47.0%	13.5%
	True Vote	46.5%	49.6%	3.9%
Votes	6,115,402	2,845,471	3,034,100	235,831

Arizona True Vote Model- Party-ID

Exit Poll	Pct	Clinton	Trump	Johnson	Stein	Other
Dem	28%	89%	7%	3%	0	1%
Rep	32%	7%	88%	3%	0	2%
Ind	40%	49%	45%	3%	2%	1%
Match	100%	46.8%	48.1%	3.0%	0.8%	1%
Unadjusted	100%	46.8%	48.2%	3.0%	0.8%	1.2%
Votes	2,573	1,204	1,240	77	21	31
		Margin	36	1.4%		

Reported	Pct	Clinton	Trump	Johnson	Stein	Other
Dem	28%	89%	7%	3%	0	1.0%
Rep	32%	7%	88%	3%	0	2.0%
Ind	40%	45%	47%	5%	2%	1.5%
Calc	100%	45.2%	48.7%	3.8%	0.8%	1.5%
Reported	100%	45.1%	48.7%	4.1%	1.3%	0.7%
Votes	2,573	1,161	1,252	106	34	19
		Margin	91	3.5%		

TRUE	Adj	Clinton	Trump	Johnson	Stein	Other
Dem	22.8%	89%	7%	3%	0	1.0%
Rep	27.4%	7%	88%	3%	0	2.0%
Ind	49.8%	45%	47%	5%	2%	1.5%
TVM1	100%	44.6%	48.8%	3.8%	0.8%	1.5%
55	95.4%	38.5%	47.3%	5.8%	2.4%	1.5%
TVM	100%	39.6%	50.7%	5.3%	3.0%	1.5%
Votes	2,573	1,019	1,305	135	77	39
		Margin	286	8.8%		

Arizona True Vote Model- Returning Voters

Recorded Vote

2012	Pct	Clinton	Trump	Other	
Obama	36.3%	91.0%	5.0%	4.0%	
Romney	43.7%	8.0%	88.0%	4.0%	
Other	1.4%	20.0%	20.0%	60.0%	
DNV (new)	18.5%	44.8%	43.7%	11.6%	Margin
	Recorded	45.13%	48.67%	6.2%	3.5%
Votes	2,573,165	1,161,351	1,252,314	159,500	90,963

TRUE VOTE

2012	Pct	Clinton	Trump	Other	
Obama	34.0%	91.0%	5.0%	4.0%	
Romney	43.7%	8.0%	88.0%	4.0%	
Other	1.4%	20.0%	20.0%	60.0%	
DNV (new)	20.8%	45%	49%	6%	Margin
	True Vote	44.1%	50.6%	5.3%	6.4%
Votes	2,573,165	1,136,052	1,301,772	135,341	165,721

New York True Vote Model- Party-ID

Exit Poll		Pct	Clinton	Trump	Stein
Dem		48%	92%	7%	1%
Rep		26%	9%	89%	2%
Ind		26%	36%	51%	13%
Match		100%	55.9%	39.8%	4.4%
Unadjusted		100%	55.8%	39.8%	4.4%
Votes		7,456	4,160	2,967	328
			Margin	-1,193	-16.0%

Reported	Pct		Clinton	Trump	Stein
Dem	48%		92%	7%	1%
Rep	26%		9%	89%	2%
Ind	26%		50%	39%	11%
Calc	100%		59.5%	36.6%	3.9%
Reported	100%		59.6%	36.7%	2.3%
Votes	7456		4,441	2,739	171
			Margin	-1,703	-22.8%

True	Adj		Clinton	Trump	Stein
Dem	39%		92%	7%	1%
Rep	19%		9%	89%	2%
Ind	42%		50%	39%	11%
TVM1	100%		58.6%	36.0%	5.4%
86	92.3%		49.6%	37.7%	5.0%
TVM	100.0%		51.5%	43.5%	5.0%
Votes	7,456		3,842	3,241	372
			Margin	-601	-11.9%

New York True Vote Model- Returning Voters

Recorded

2012	Pct	Clinton	Trump	Other	
Obama	54.9%	92.0%	6.0%	2.0%	
Romney	30.5%	8.0%	89.0%	3.0%	
Other	1.3%	20.0%	20.0%	60.0%	
DNV (new)	13.4%	48.0%	43.0%	9.0%	Margin
	Recorded	59.6%	36.4%	4.0%	23.2%
Votes	7,455,767	4,443,488	2,715,075	297,204	1,728,413

TRUE VOTE

2012	Pct	Clinton	Trump	Other	
Obama	51.4%	92.0%	6.0%	2.0%	
Romney	30.5%	8.0%	89.0%	3.0%	
Other	1.3%	20.0%	20.0%	60.0%	
DNV (new)	16.8%	48.0%	43.0%	9.0%	Margin
	True Vote	58.1%	37.7%	4.2%	20.4%
Votes	7,455,767	4,329,801	2,810,675	315,291	1,519,126

Texas True Vote Model- Returning Voters

Exit Poll	Pct	Clinton	Trump	Johnson	Stein	Other
Dem	29%	93%	5%	1%	1%	0%
Rep	38%	9%	88%	2%	0%	1%
Ind	33%	36%	51%	7%	2%	4%
Match	100%	42.3%	51.7%	3.4%	1.0%	2%
Unadjusted	100%	42.3%	51.8%	4.9%	0.90%	0.1%
Votes	8,969	3,794	4,646	439	81	9.0
		Margin	852	9.5%		

Reported	Pct	Clinton	Trump	Johnson	Stein	Other
Dem	29%	93%	5%	1%	1%	0.0%
Rep	38%	9%	88%	2%	0%	1.0%
Ind	33%	39%	52%	7%	2%	0.0%
Calc	100%	43.3%	52.1%	3.4%	1.0%	0.4%
Reported	100%	43.2%	52.2%	3.2%	0.8%	0.6%
Votes	8,969	3,878	4,685	283	72	51
		Margin	807	9.0%		

True	Adj	Clinton	Trump	Johnson	Stein	Other
Dem	29.2%	93%	5%	1%	1%	0.0%
Rep	32.6%	9%	88%	2%	0%	1.0%
Ind	38.2%	39%	52%	7%	2%	0.0%
TVM1	100.0%	45.0%	50.0%	3.6%	1.1%	0.3%
TVM	100.0%	41.7%	50.9%	5.1%	2.0%	0.3%
Votes	8,969	3,737	4,567	453	183	29
		Margin	830	6.8%		

Texas True Vote Model- Returning Voters

Recorded Vote

2012	Pct	Clinton	Trump	Other	
Obama	33.6%	92.0%	5.0%	3.0%	
Romney	46.5%	8.0%	90.0%	2.0%	
Other	1.2%	20.0%	20.0%	60.0%	
DNV (new)	18.7%	44.5%	45.0%	10.5%	Margin
	Recorded	43.2%	52.2%	4.6%	8.9%
Votes	8,969,226	3,877,282	4,678,390	413,553	801,108

TRUE VOTE

2012	Pct	Clinton	Trump	Other	
Obama	31.5%	92.0%	5.0%	3.0%	
Romney	46.5%	8.0%	90.0%	2.0%	
Other	1.2%	20.0%	20.0%	60.0%	
DNV (new)	20.8%	44.5%	45.0%	10.5%	Margin
	True Vote	42.2%	53.0%	4.8%	10.8%
Votes	8,969,226	3,786,772	4,754,609	427,845	967,837

Illinois True Vote Model- Party-ID

Exit Poll	Pct	Clinton	Trump	Johnson	Stein	Other
Dem	45%	93%	5%	1%	0%	1%
Rep	30%	8%	88%	3%	1%	0%
Ind	25%	37%	39%	9%	4%	11%
Match	100%	53.5%	38.4%	3.6%	1.3%	3%
Unadjusted	100%	53.6%	38.4%	4.9%	0.90%	2%
Votes	5,536	2,968	2,126	271	50	122
		Margin	-842	-15.2%		

Reported	Pct	Clinton	Trump	Johnson	Stein	Other
Dem	45%	93%	5%	1%	0%	1%
Rep	30%	8%	88%	3%	1%	0%
Ind	25%	44%	43%	9%	4%	0%
Calc	100%	55.3%	39.4%	3.6%	1.3%	0.4%
Reported	100%	55.8%	38.8%	3.8%	1.4%	0.2%
Votes	5,536	3,091	2,146	210	77	13
		Margin	-945	-17.1%		

TRUE	Adj	Clinton	Trump	Johnson	Stein	Other
Dem	37.1%	93%	5%	1%	0%	1%
Rep	27.8%	8%	88%	3%	1%	0%
Ind	35.1%	41%	43%	9%	4%	3%
TVM1	100.0%	51.1%	41.4%	4.4%	1.7%	1.4%
TVM	100.0%	46.9%	45.0%	4.7%	2.0%	1.4%
Votes	5,536	2,594	2,491	260	113	78
		Margin	-103	-3.4%		

Illinois True Vote Model- Returning Voters

Recorded Vote

2012	Pct	Clinton	Trump	Other	
Obama	49.7%	90.0%	5.0%	5.0%	
Romney	35.2%	9.0%	87.0%	4.0%	
Other	1.4%	20.0%	20.0%	60.0%	
DNV (new)	13.6%	55.5%	40.0%	4.5%	Margin
	Recorded	55.8%	38.8%	5.4%	17.0%
Votes	5,536,424	3,089,012	2,150,059	297,352	938,953

TRUE VOTE

2012	Pct	Clinton	Trump	Other	
Obama	46.6%	90.0%	5.0%	5.0%	
Romney	35.2%	9.0%	87.0%	4.0%	
Other	1.4%	20.0%	20.0%	60.0%	
DNV (new)	16.8%	55.5%	40.0%	4.5%	Margin
	True Vote	54.7%	39.9%	5.4%	14.8%
Votes	5,536,424	3,029,009	2,210,933	296,483	818,076

D. An Open Source Solution

Posters who claim that technology can never guarantee that our elections will be honest are missing the overall by focusing on only one factor in the equation. They claim that any system can be hacked (which is true) – but they leave it at that. They fail to consider that technology, used in conjunction with low-tech hand-counts, provides a more secure voting system than hand-counts alone.

Current voting systems are designed to be hacked. We need systems that are designed to work. It's that simple. Data redundancy, auditable processes, open source code, non-proprietary systems, expert design (not r/w hacks), voters can confirm their own vote. What's wrong with that? Let experts check the code and agree that it would work. As expert Steve Spoonamore has said: you just need to make sure that 1+1=2. It's not rocket science. If voters have the ability to check their vote after it has been transmitted to a tabulator and find a mistake, they can report it. It is a citizen auditable process. It's just common sense.

We are the voters. We own the hardware. We own the software. We check our votes. This way we have the best of both worlds: A HYBRID system of hand-counted ballot summaries posted for viewing at the precinct as well as on the Internet. Each ballot contains an anonymous voter code. Privacy is not an issue; the voters can check their votes online. It is a self-auditing system. The key is data redundancy and transparency– and that is why an Open Source/Internet system can provide a solution. The Diebold and ES&S voting machines and central tabulators use proprietary code for one reason: they are designed to be manipulated. Non-proprietary hardware and Open Source software is the solution, not the current systems from right-wing corporations that steal elections while Congress looks the other way.

Spoonamore is allowed to analyze Diebold ATM software, but prohibited from looking at Diebold's voting machine code. He says that each voter should be allowed to check their vote electronically on the County Web site. That is exactly what I have been saying all along. He agrees with my contention that Open Source is a must. He calls it "freeware". Same thing.

Spoonamore says that the software should be made available for free. What he doesn't say is that there would be an additional benefit: there could be no bribing of election officials to install unverifiable machines that have consistently failed inspection procedures.

The solution is simple, so simple that it has never been and will never be proposed by corrupt politicians and election officials. The use of current closed systems by election officials and their refusal to consider an Open Source solution is itself proof that it would work. Virtually all voters would have online access to their vote. And many would check to see that it was correct. They would in effect be auditing and exit polling themselves.

To the skeptics: True Vote count = hand-vote count at the voting site
To the technologists: True Vote count = hand-vote count (posted at the voting site) + voter-verified tabulation on the Internet of ALL precincts

Technology skeptics offer no solution, just the mantra that our best technology is incapable of insuring fair elections – and that every system can be hacked. They fail to consider the primary goal of any security system: data redundancy and built-in safeguards to detect fraud. The skeptics speak with a tone of final authority. But how do they know a nearly foolproof system cannot be developed?

Why not create a prototype? Refusal to even consider that a technical solution could enhance hand-counting ballots only serves to enable the corruption. But what if the experts can provide such a hybrid solution? Would they accept it?

Why do the skeptics display the arrogance of supreme authority? Why do they continue to pontificate their version of the Ultimate Truth? Who are they to say that TECHNOLOGY would never work; that corrupt election officials can never be outsmarted by experts in computer security and software design; that non-proprietary, robust hardware/software based election systems would never work? How do they know that? What is their motive in promoting the myth that technology could never work?

The fault lies not in our technology, but in our FAILURE to apply it to solve THE problem.

One skeptic claimed that those who believed that technology would work "refuse to see that transparency, simplicity, comprehension and control of the electoral process by the citizen-voters is essential to their opponents' view of what is required for democratic process, and that no technologically sophisticated "solution" can satisfy those requirements".

He has it exactly backwards. An Open Source system is the only one which provides full transparency that voters can have confidence in because they would own the machines and the software and could verify that their votes (and those of others) have been counted correctly.

The poster adds that voting systems are unlike other "systems under the operational control of the institutions that maintains a stake in those systems operating properly for the benefit of those institutions, and that the electoral process by its nature is one of divided interests. (Power tends to corrupt, and absolute power corrupts absolutely.)"

He misses the essential point that the problem lies not in technology, but in those who have the power to use it and fail to do so. I have said that a voting system could be designed such that the probability would be extremely low that corrupt election officials and hackers would succeed in miscounting the votes.

Election officials have zero knowledge of technology. They are not even good at hiding their transparent efforts in Wisconsin of stuffing ballot bags or stacking 50 ballots in a row for the Republican in a city that voted 67% for his opponent. A robust, transparent, data redundant system would never allow these amateurish anomalies. In the highly unlikely event that a hacker was able to break into the Internet database, it would be obvious: the totals would not match the precinct-posted hard copy and the voters own copy.

The skeptic goes on to say: "I'm sure that I could design a electronic voting system that is guaranteed to work properly if I could continue to control all the actors and all the checks and balances along the way — and if I stayed honest — but so what? Why should voters want or need such a system?"

"There is no reason for voters to trust me, and even if they did the system (not their method for "checking" how their vote was counter) would remain opaque to them, and there would be no trace of collective participatory democracy in the vote counting process, which like the so-called negativists I consider important, if not essential, to the process".

Even if he could design such a system, why would he want to do it all by himself? Why not collaborate with other experts who could check his design? Would he be willing to test a prototype? Even if it is "opaque" to voters as he calls it, the only relevant question is: would it solve the problem? That is all that matters. Does he really believe that voters care to know the details of how the system is designed? Do they have a clue as to how their financial transactions are processed?

Of course there is no reason to trust him; that's why he would have to work with a team of professionals in designing the system. There is no reason for voters to trust him if others cannot revue his code to make sure that 1+1 is always equal to 2 and that there is never a reduction in the vote count.

He states that there would be no trace of collective participation in the vote-counting process – and in so doing contradicts himself. Voters would participate by checking to make sure that votes posted on the wall of their precinct match the votes uploaded to the Internet. There is no way that they can do that using current voting systems. But they could if they had a copy of their ballot and were able to check that it was properly recorded on the Net. That is quite an improvement over the current "system".

Another skeptic asked: "And exactly how would this stop ballot box stuffing? Ghost voters do NOT check their ballots on the internet. Counting the hard copy ballots at the precinct that the voters marked. Counting the night of the election while ballots are still in full view and custody of numerous observers — that isn't simple? Guess not".

Voters would be assigned sequential IDs on the ballots that would be recorded in poll books. A summary of votes cast would be posted periodically on the precinct wall by Voter ID. The number of entries in the poll book would have to match the posted summary. The corresponding ballot records would be uploaded to the Internet – where they are also sorted by Voter ID. The number of ballot data records in the Internet precinct database would have to match the posted summary at the precinct.

The poster forgets that total votes cast must be tabulated for each precinct in each county. Who would do the tabulation? Would it be done by hand calculator or abacus or computer? How would voters know that their vote and those of other voters in all other precincts would be tabulated correctly? Where would they go to check their vote other than on the precinct wall? There is just one feasible location where they could check that their vote was tabulated correctly: on the Internet. Can the poster provide an alternative? Or would he just trust that the thousands of hand-counted locations were tabulated correctly – and that there was a perfect chain-of-custody?

E. An Internet Crank

Roger Stone wrote "**Can the 2016 election be rigged? You bet!** "in
The Hill

Donald Trump has said publicly that he fears the next election will be rigged. Based both on technical capability and recent history, Trump's concerns are not unfounded. A recent study by Stanford University proved that Hillary Clinton's campaign rigged the system to steal the nomination from Bernie Sanders. What was done to Bernie Sanders in Wisconsin is stunning. Why would the Clintons not cheat again?

The issue here is both voter fraud, which is limited but does happen, and election theft through the manipulation of the computerized voting machines, particularly the DIEBOLD/PES voting machines in wide usage in most states.

POLITICO profiled a Princeton professor who has demonstrated how the electronic voting machines that are most widely used can be hacked in five minutes or less! Robert Fitrakis Professor of Political Science in the Social and Behavioral Sciences Department at Columbus State Community College has written a must-read book on the strip and flip technique used to rig these machines. Professor Fitrakis is a Green Party activist..

To be very clear both parties have engaged in this skullduggery and it is the party in power in each state that has custody of the machines and control of their programing. This year, the results of machines in Pennsylvania, Virginia and Ohio, where Governor John Kasich controls the machines, must be matched with exit polls, for example.

How do the pols of both parties do it? Simply have the votes for the other guy be given to your guy and vice versa. You keep the total vote the same. Europe has rejected electronic voting machines because they are untrustworthy. This is not a secret. The media continues a drum beat insisting voter fraud is non-existent without ever addressing the more ominous question of manipulation of the voting machines. It keeps those in control in control.

Additionally some states still use machines that include no paper trail. The "evidence" is destroyed. In Europe, they use exit polling to determine who won and lost. The tabulated vote only serves as a formal verification. But that is done with paper ballots and hand counts under supervision, the way we used to do it.

Here's the recipe now: (1) Publish a poll contrived to suggest the result you are going to bring about.   (2) Manipulate the machines to bring about precisely your desired outcome.

Mathematician and voting statistic expert Richard Charnin has produced a compelling study by comparing polling to actual results and exit polls to make a compelling case for voting machine manipulation in the Badger state.

When the Trump vs. Cruz primary took place, the same pattern emerged again of a Marquette University poll showing a 20 point shift from Trump ahead by 10% to Trump behind by 10%, which was simply absurd. Shifts like that don't happen over brief intervals of time, absent a nuclear explosion. It didn't make any sense - unless you knew what was going on was an "instant replay" of Walker's victories. The machine Priebus built was delivering for Cruz big time.

The polling industry has been reported to be "in a state of crisis" because they are altering their samples to favor Hillary. The Reuters poll actually got busted for oversampling Democrats in order to inflate Hillary's lead.. In fact, post-convention polling for the Trump effort by pollster Tony Fabrizio in key swing states was encouraging. Perhaps this is why the establishment elites have gone into over-drive to attack Trump.

Hillary hasn't exactly had smooth sailing. Julian Assange of Wikileaks said he had inconvertible proof that as Secretary of State Hillary Clinton armed

Isis LINK. The IRS has opened an investigation to the Clinton Foundation and it's many offshoots, and Hillary got caught lying about what FBI Director Comey did say about her.

But you will see less of Hillary's problems in the mainstream media, which has gone completely overboard in its relentless, even hysterical, efforts to lambaste Trump and promote her. Every remotely objective commentator has been stunned. Trump will, however, have an opportunity to drive these points home in the debates.

We are now living in a fake reality of constructed data and phony polls. The computerized voting machines can be hacked and rigged and after the experience of Bernie Sanders there is no reason to believe they won't be. Don't be taken in.

Felix Salmon in *Splinter News*: Is the Donald Trump campaign weaponizing a left-wing internet crank?

*The ever-controversial political strategist Roger Stone caused a lot of predictable headlines this week when he **said** there would be a "bloodbath" were Hillary Clinton to be sworn in as president. What got less attention was the chain of his logic. Stone thinks that if Trump fails to win the presidential election that will be because Hillary Clinton stole it. He explains: "If there's voter fraud, this election will be illegitimate, the election of the winner will be illegitimate, we will have a constitutional crisis, widespread civil disobedience, and the government will no longer be the government. Stone, here, is putting into words the kind of reaction that Donald Trump wants all of his supporters to feel whenever he **rails against election fraud.***

*Stone and Trump base most of their argument, such that it is, on one man. Stone refers to him as "a mathematician called Richard Charnin." For years now, Charnin has been best known as the go-to guy for anybody who wants evidence that voter fraud is deciding elections. He's beloved in the corner of the internet which believes that Hillary Clinton **stole the Democratic nomination** from Bernie Sanders, or, for that matter, that George W*

*Bush **stole the 2004 election** from John Kerry. When he's not concentrating on who-killed-JFK conspiracy theories, he can generally be relied upon to say that the more left-wing candidate got more votes than the winner in major elections.*

That makes Charnin a very strange bedfellow for the Trump campaign, just in terms of his political leanings. But even stranger is the idea that Trump would want his supporters to pick up Charnin's voter fraud ball and run it all the way into the zone of democratic illegitimacy. And yet here we have a high-profile Trump surrogate (and former Nixon adviser) talking about some kind of popular insurrection should the election not break his way. Even Charnin himself doesn't go that far: while he'll happily say that many elections have been "stolen", he doesn't go on to say that if you stole an election then that makes your presidency illegitimate, or that it is incumbent upon the populace to shut any such president's government down.

*Charnin is a pretty standard-issue internet crank; his speciality is looking at the difference between election results and exit polls, and determining that the exit polls somehow do a better job of reflecting the will of the people than fully-tallied results. (**They don't**.) On his own,*

*Charnin is mostly harmless. **His accusations are serious**, but they have never come close to being proved, and until they are proved true, they should properly carry no political consequence. Roger Stone, however, has decided that the time has come to weaponize Charnin, and to use his theories as being, on their face, sufficient reason to bring down an elected government. If that isn't treason, it's very close. Is it too much to hope that Charnin will denounce him?*

F. Exposed: The Russian 'DNC Hack' Myth

On January 17, 2017, U.S. intelligence, military and diplomatic veterans called on President Obama to release the evidence backing up allegations that Russia aided the Trump campaign – or admit that the proof is lacking.

MEMORANDUM FOR: President Barack Obama

FROM: Veteran Intelligence Professionals for Sanity (VIPS)

SUBJECT: A Key Issue That Still Needs to be Resolved

As President-elect Donald Trump prepares to take the oath of office Friday, a pall hangs over his upcoming presidency amid an unprecedentedly concerted campaign to delegitimize it. Unconfirmed accusations continue to swirl alleging that Russian President Vladimir Putin authorized "Russian hacking" that helped put Mr. Trump in the White House.

As President for a few more days, you have the power to demand concrete evidence of a link between the Russians and WikiLeaks, which published the bulk of the information in question. Lacking that evidence, the American people should be told that there is no fire under the smoke and mirrors of recent weeks.

We urge you to authorize public release of any tangible evidence that takes us beyond the unsubstantiated, "we-assess" judgments by the intelligence agencies. Otherwise, we – as well as other skeptical Americans – will be left with the corrosive suspicion that the intense campaign of accusations is part of a wider attempt to discredit the Russians and those – like Mr. Trump – who wish to deal constructively with them.

Remember the Maine?

Alleged Russian interference has been labeled "an act of war" and Mr. Trump a "traitor." But the "intelligence" served up to support those charges does not pass the smell test. Your press conference on Wednesday will give you a chance to respond more persuasively to NBC's Peter Alexander's challenge at the last one (on Dec. 16) "to show the proof [and], as they say, put your money where your mouth is and declassify some of the intelligence. ..."

You told Alexander you were reluctant to "compromise sources and methods." We can understand that concern better than most Americans. We would remind you, though, that at critical junctures in the past, your predecessors made judicious decisions to give higher priority to buttressing the credibility of U.S. intelligence-based policy than to protecting sources and methods. With the Kremlin widely accused by politicians and pundits of "an act of war," this is the kind of textbook case in which you might seriously consider taking special pains to substantiate serious allegations with hard intelligence – if there is any.

During the Cuban missile crisis, for instance, President Kennedy ordered us to show highly classified photos of Soviet nuclear missiles in Cuba and on ships en route, even though this blew sensitive detail regarding the imagery intelligence capabilities of the cameras on our U-2 aircraft.

President Ronald Reagan's reaction to the Libyan terrorist bombing of La Belle Disco in Berlin on April 5, 1986, that killed two and injured 79 other U.S. servicemen is another case in point. We had intercepted a Libyan message that morning: "At 1:30 in the morning one of the acts was carried out with success, without leaving a trace behind." (We should add here that NSA's dragnet SIGINT capability 30 years later renders it virtually impossible to avoid "leaving a trace behind" once a message is put on the network.)

President Reagan ordered the U.S. Air Force to bomb Col. Muammar Qaddafi's palace compound to smithereens, killing several civilians. Amid widespread international consternation and demands for proof that Libya was responsible for the Berlin attack, President Reagan ordered us to make public the encrypted Libyan message, thereby sacrificing a collection/decryption capability unknown to the Libyans – until then.

As senior CIA veteran Milton Bearden has put it, there are occasions when more damage is done by "protecting" sources and methods than by revealing them.

Where's the Beef?

We find the New York Times- and Washington Post-led media Blitz against Trump and Putin truly extraordinary, despite our long experience with intelligence/media related issues. On Jan. 6, the day after your top intelligence officials published what we found to be an embarrassingly shoddy report purporting to prove Russian hacking in support of Trump's candidacy, the Times banner headline across all six columns on page 1 read: "**PUTIN LED SCHEME TO AID TRUMP, REPORT SAYS.**"

The lead article began: "President Vladimir V. Putin of Russia directed a vast cyberattack aimed at denying Hillary Clinton the presidency and installing Donald J. Trump in the Oval Office, the nation's top intelligence agencies said in an extraordinary report they delivered on Friday to Mr. Trump." Eschewing all subtlety, the Times added that the revelations in "this damning report … undermined the legitimacy" of the President-elect, and "made the case that Mr. Trump was the favored candidate of Mr. Putin."

On page A10, however, Times investigative reporter Scott Shane pointed out: "What is missing from the public report is what many Americans most eagerly anticipated: hard evidence to back up the agencies' claims that the Russian government engineered the election attack. That is a significant omission."

Shane continued, "Instead, the message from the agencies essentially amounts to 'trust us.' There is no discussion of the forensics used to recognize the handiwork of known hacking groups, no mention of intercepted communications between the Kremlin and the hackers, no hint of spies reporting from inside Moscow's propaganda machinery."

Shane added that the intelligence report "offers an obvious reason for leaving out the details, declaring that including 'the precise bases for its assessments' would 'reveal sensitive sources and methods and imperil the ability to collect critical foreign intelligence in the future.'"

Shane added a quote from former National Security Agency lawyer Susan Hennessey: "The unclassified report is underwhelming at best. There is essentially no new information for those who have been paying attention." Ms. Hennessey served as an attorney in NSA's Office of General Counsel and is now a Brookings Fellow in National Security Law.

Everyone Hacks

There is a lot of ambiguity – whether calculated or not – about "Russian hacking." "Everyone knows that everyone hacks," says everyone: Russia hacks; China hacks; every nation that can hacks. So do individuals of various nationalities. This is not the question.

You said at your press conference on Dec. 16 "the intelligence that I have seen gives me great confidence in their [U.S. intelligence agencies'] assessment that the Russians carried out this hack." "Which hack?" you were asked. "The hack of the DNC and the hack of John Podesta," you answered.

Earlier during the press conference you alluded to the fact that "the information was in the hands of WikiLeaks." The key question is how the material from "Russian hacking" got to WikiLeaks, because it was WikiLeaks that published the DNC and Podesta emails.

Our VIPS colleague William Binney, who was Technical Director of NSA and created many of the collection systems still in use, assures us that NSA's "cast-iron" coverage – particularly surrounding Julian Assange and other people associated with WikiLeaks – would almost certainly have yielded a record of any electronic transfer from Russia to WikiLeaks. Binney has used some of the highly classified slides released by Edward Snowden to demonstrate precisely how NSA accomplishes this using trace mechanisms embedded throughout the network. [See: **"U.S. Intel Vets Dispute Russia Hacking Claims,"** Dec. 12, 2016.]

NSA Must Come Clean

We strongly suggest that you ask NSA for any evidence it may have indicating that the results of Russian hacking were given to WikiLeaks. If NSA can produce such evidence, you may wish to order whatever declassification may be needed and then release the evidence. This would go a long way toward allaying suspicions that no evidence exists. If NSA cannot give you that information – and quickly – this would probably mean it does not have any.

In all candor, the checkered record of Director of National Intelligence James Clapper for trustworthiness makes us much less confident that anyone should take it on faith that he is more "trustworthy than the Russians," as you suggested on Dec. 16. You will probably recall that Clapper lied under oath to the Senate Intelligence Committee on March 12, 2013, about NSA dragnet activities; later apologizing for testimony he admitted had been "clearly erroneous." **In our Memorandum for you on Dec. 11, 2013, we cited chapter and verse as to why Clapper should have been fired for saying things he knew to** be "clearly erroneous."

In that Memorandum, we endorsed the demand by Rep. Jim Sensenbrenner that Clapper be removed. "Lying to Congress is a federal offense, and Clapper ought to be fired and prosecuted for it," said Sensenbrenner in an interview with The Hill. "The only way laws are effective is if they're enforced."

Actually, we have had trouble understanding why, almost four years after he deliberately misled the Senate, Clapper remains Director of National Intelligence – overseeing the entire intelligence community.

Hacks or Leaks?

Not mentioned until now is our conclusion that leaks are the source of the WikiLeaks disclosures in question – not hacking. Leaks normally leave no electronic trace. William Binney has been emphasizing this for several months and suggesting strongly that the disclosures were from a leaker with physical access to the information – not a hacker with only remote access.

**This, of course, makes it even harder to pin the blame on President Putin, or anyone else. And we suspect that this explains why NSA demurred when asked to join the CIA and FBI in expressing "high confidence" in this key judgment of the report put out under Clapper's auspices on Jan. 6, yielding this curious formulation:

"We also assess Putin and the Russian Government aspired to help President-elect Trump's election chances when possible by discrediting Secretary Clinton and publicly contrasting her unfavorably to him. All three agencies agree with this judgment. CIA and FBI have high confidence in this judgment; NSA has moderate confidence." (Emphasis, and lack of emphasis, in original)

In addition, former U.K. Ambassador Craig Murray has said publicly he has first-hand information on the provenance of the leaks, and has expressed surprise that no one from the New York Times or the Washington Post has tried to get in touch with him. We would be interested in knowing whether anyone from your administration, including the intelligence community, has made any effort to contact Ambassador Murray.

What to Do

President-elect Trump said a few days ago that his team will have a "full report on hacking within 90 days." Whatever the findings of the

Trump team turn out to be, they will no doubt be greeted with due skepticism, since Mr. Trump is in no way a disinterested party.

You, on the other hand, enjoy far more credibility – AND power – for the next few days. And we assume you would not wish to hobble your successor with charges that cannot withstand close scrutiny. We suggest you order the chiefs of the NSA, FBI and CIA to the White House and ask them to lay all their cards on the table. They need to show you why you should continue to place credence in what, a month ago, you described as "uniform intelligence assessments" about Russian hacking.

At that point, if the intelligence heads have credible evidence, you have the option of ordering it released – even at the risk of damage to sources and methods. For what it may be worth, we will not be shocked if it turns out that they can do no better than the evidence-deprived assessments they have served up in recent weeks. In that case, we would urge you, in all fairness, to let the American people in on the dearth of convincing evidence before you leave office.

As you will have gathered by now, we strongly suspect that the evidence your intelligence chiefs have of a joint **RUSSIAN-HACKING-WIKILEAKS-PUBLISHING** operation is no better than the "intelligence" evidence in 2002-2003 – expressed then with comparable flat-fact "certitude" – of the existence of weapons of mass destruction in Iraq.

Obama's Legacy

Mr. President, there is much talk in your final days in office about your legacy. Will part of that legacy be that you stood by while flames of illegitimacy rose willy-nilly around your successor? Or will you use your power to reveal the information – or the fact that there are merely unsupported allegations – that would enable us to deal with them responsibly?

In the immediate wake of the holiday on which we mark the birthday of Dr. Martin Luther King, Jr., it seems appropriate to make reference to his legacy, calling to mind the graphic words in his "Letter from the Birmingham City Jail," with which he reminds us of our common duty to expose lies and injustice:

"LIKE A BOIL THAT CAN NEVER BE CURED AS LONG AS IT IS COVERED UP, BUT MUST BE OPENED WITH ALL ITS PUS-FLOWING UGLINESS TO THE NATURAL MEDICINES OF AIR AND LIGHT, INJUSTICE MUST LIKEWISE BE EXPOSED, WITH ALL OF THE TENSION ITS EXPOSING CREATES, TO THE LIGHT OF HUMAN CONSCIENCE AND THE AIR OF NATIONAL OPINION BEFORE IT CAN BE CURED."

FOR THE STEERING GROUP, VETERAN INTELLIGENCE PROFESSIONALS FOR SANITY (VIPS)

William Binney, former Technical Director, World Geopolitical & Military Analysis, NSA; co-founder, SIGINT Automation Research Center (ret.)

Marshall Carter-Tripp, Foreign Service Officer (ret) and former Office Director in the State Department Bureau of Intelligence and Research

Thomas Drake, former Senior Executive, NSA

Bogdan Dzakovic, Former Team Leader of Federal Air Marshals and Red Team, FAA Security, (ret.) (associate VIPS)

Philip Giraldi, CIA, Operations Officer (ret.)

Mike Gravel, former Adjutant, top secret control officer, Communications Intelligence Service; special agent of the Counter Intelligence Corps and former United States Senator

Matthew Hoh, former Capt., USMC, Iraq & Foreign Service Officer, Afghanistan (associate VIPS)

Larry Johnson, former CIA Intelligence Officer & former State Department Counter-Terrorism Official, ret.

Michael S. Kearns, Captain, USAF (Ret.); ex-Master SERE Instructor for Strategic Reconnaissance Ops (NSA/DIA) and Special Mission Units (JSOC)

Brady Kiesling, former U.S. Foreign Service Officer, ret.(Assoc. VIPS)

John Kiriakou, Former CIA Counterterrorism Officer and former Senior Investigator, Senate Foreign Relations Committee

Karen Kwiatkowski, former Lt. Col., US Air Force (ret.), at Office of Secretary of Defense watching the lies on Iraq, 2001-03

Linda Lewis, WMD preparedness policy analyst, USDA (ret.)

David MacMichael, National Intelligence Council (ret.)

Ray McGovern, US Army infantry/intelligence, CIA analyst (ret.)

Todd E. Pierce, MAJ, US Army Judge Advocate (ret.)

Elizabeth Murray, former Deputy National Intelligence Officer for Middle East, CIA (ret.)

Scott Ritter, former MAJ., USMC, former UN Weapon Inspector, Iraq

Coleen Rowley, FBI Special Agent and former Minneapolis Division Legal Counsel (ret.)

Peter Van Buren, U.S. Dept. of State, Foreign Service Officer (ret.) (associate VIPS)

Kirk Wiebe, former Senior Analyst, SIGINT Automation Research Center, NSA (ret.)

Robert Wing, former Foreign Service Officer (associate VIPS)

Ann Wright, U.S. Army Reserve Colonel (ret) , former U.S. Diplomat

On July 24, 2017 in a memo to President Trump, VIPS cited new forensic studies to challenge the claim of the key Jan. 6 "assessment" that Russia "hacked" Democratic emails last year.

MEMORANDUM FOR: The President

FROM: Veteran Intelligence Professionals for Sanity (VIPS)

SUBJECT: Was the "Russian Hack" an Inside Job?

EXECUTIVE SUMMARY

Forensic studies of "Russian hacking" into Democratic National Committee computers last year reveal that on July 5, 2016, data was **LEAKED (NOT HACKED)** by a person with physical access to DNC computer. After examining metadata from the "Guccifer 2.0" July 5, 2016 intrusion into the DNC server, independent cyber investigators have concluded that an insider copied DNC data onto an external storage device.

Key among the findings of the independent forensic investigations is the conclusion that the DNC data was copied onto a storage device **AT A SPEED THAT FAR EXCEEDS AN INTERNET CAPABILITY FOR A REMOTE HACK**. Of equal importance, the forensics show that the copying was performed on the East coast of the U.S. Thus far, mainstream media have ignored the findings of these independent **studies [see here and here]**.

Independent analyst Skip Folden, who retired after 25 years as the IBM Program Manager for Information Technology, US, who examined the recent forensic findings, is a co-author of this Memorandum. He has drafted a more detailed technical report titled "Cyber-Forensic Investigation of 'Russian Hack' and Missing Intelligence Community Disclaimers," and sent it to the offices of the Special Counsel and the Attorney General. VIPS member William Binney, a former Technical Director at the National Security Agency, and other senior NSA "alumni" in VIPS attest to the professionalism of the independent forensic findings.

The recent forensic studies fill in a critical gap. Why the FBI neglected to perform any independent forensics on the original "Guccifer 2.0" material remains a mystery – as does the lack of any sign that the "hand-picked analysts" from the FBI, CIA, and NSA, who wrote the "Intelligence Community Assessment" dated January 6, 2017, gave any attention to forensics.

NOTE: There has been so much conflation of charges about hacking that we wish to make very clear the primary focus of this Memorandum. We focus specifically on the July 5, 2016 alleged Guccifer 2.0 "hack" of the DNC server. In earlier VIPS memoranda we addressed the lack of any evidence connecting the Guccifer 2.0 alleged hacks and WikiLeaks, and we asked President Obama specifically to disclose any evidence that WikiLeaks received DNC data from the Russians [see here and here].

Addressing this point at his last press conference (January 18), he described "the conclusions of the intelligence community" as "not conclusive," even though the Intelligence Community Assessment of January 6 expressed "high confidence" that Russian intelligence "relayed material it acquired from the DNC … to WikiLeaks."

Obama's admission came as no surprise to us. It has long been clear to us that the reason the U.S. government lacks conclusive evidence of a transfer of a "Russian hack" to WikiLeaks is because there was no such transfer. Based mostly on the cumulatively unique technical experience of our ex-NSA colleagues, we have been saying for almost a year that the DNC data reached WikiLeaks via a copy/leak by a DNC insider (but almost certainly not the same person who copied DNC data on July 5, 2016).

From the information available, we conclude that the same inside-DNC, copy/leak PROCESS was used at two different times, by two different entities, for two distinctly different purposes:

(1) an inside leak to WikiLeaks before Julian Assange announced on June 12, 2016, that he had DNC documents and planned to publish

them (which he did on July 22) – the presumed objective being to expose strong DNC bias toward the Clinton candidacy; and (2) a separate leak on July 5, 2016, to pre-emptively taint anything WikiLeaks might later publish by "showing" it came from a "Russian hack."

Mr. President:

This is our first VIPS Memorandum for you, but we have a history of letting U.S. Presidents know when we think our former intelligence colleagues have gotten something important wrong, and why. For example, **our first such memorandum, a same-day commentary for President George W. Bush on Colin Powell's** U.N. speech on February 5, 2003, warned that the "unintended consequences were likely to be catastrophic," should the U.S. attack Iraq and "justify" the war on intelligence that we retired intelligence officers could readily see as fraudulent and driven by a war agenda.

The January 6 "Intelligence Community Assessment" by "hand-picked" analysts from the FBI, CIA, and NSA seems to fit into the same agenda-driven category. It is largely based on an "assessment," not supported by any apparent evidence, that a shadowy entity with the moniker "Guccifer 2.0" hacked the DNC on behalf of Russian intelligence and gave DNC emails to WikiLeaks.

The recent forensic findings mentioned above have put a huge dent in that assessment and cast serious doubt on the underpinnings of the extraordinarily successful campaign to blame the Russian government for hacking. The pundits and politicians who have led the charge against Russian "meddling" in the U.S. election can be expected to try to cast doubt on the forensic findings, if they ever do bubble up into the mainstream media. But the technical limitations of today's Internet are widely understood. We are prepared to answer any substantive challenges on their merits.

You may wish to ask CIA Director Mike Pompeo what he knows about this. Our own lengthy intelligence community experience suggests that it is possible that neither former CIA Director John Brennan, nor the cyber-warriors who worked for him, have been completely candid with their new director regarding how this all went down.

Copied, Not Hacked

As indicated above, the independent forensic work just completed focused on data COPIED (NOT HACKED) by a shadowy persona named "Guccifer 2.0." The forensics reflect what seems to have been a desperate effort to "blame the Russians" for publishing highly embarrassing DNC emails three days before the Democratic convention last July. Since the content of the DNC emails reeked of pro-Clinton bias, her campaign saw an overriding need to divert attention from content to provenance – as in, who "hacked" those DNC emails? The campaign was enthusiastically supported by compliant "mainstream" media; they are still on a roll.

"The Russians" were the ideal culprit. And, after WikiLeaks editor Julian Assange announced on June 12, 2016, "We have emails related to Hillary Clinton which are pending publication," her campaign had more than a month before the convention to insert its own "forensic facts" and prime the media pump to put the blame on "Russian meddling." Mrs. Clinton's PR chief Jennifer Palmieri has explained how she used golf carts to make the rounds at the convention. She wrote that her "mission was to get the press to focus on something even we found difficult to process: the prospect that Russia had not only hacked and stolen emails from the DNC, but that it had done so to help Donald Trump and hurt Hillary Clinton."

Independent cyber-investigators have now completed the kind of forensic work that the intelligence assessment did not do. Oddly, the "hand-picked" intelligence analysts contented themselves with "assessing" this and "assessing" that. In contrast, the investigators dug deep and came up with verifiable evidence from metadata found in the record of the alleged Russian hack.

They found that the purported "hack" of the DNC by Guccifer 2.0 was not a hack, by Russia or anyone else. Rather it originated with a copy (onto an external storage device – a thumb drive, for example) by an insider. The data was leaked to implicate Russia. We do not know who or what the murky Guccifer 2.0 is. You may wish to ask the FBI.

The Time Sequence

June 12, 2016: Assange **announces** WikiLeaks is about to publish "emails related to Hillary Clinton."

June 14, 2016: DNC contractor Crowdstrike, (with a dubious **professional record and multiple conflicts** of interest) announces that malware has been found on the DNC server and claims there is evidence it was injected by Russians.

June 15, 2016: "Guccifer 2.0" affirms the DNC statement; claims responsibility for the "hack;" claims to be a WikiLeaks source; and posts a document that the forensics show was synthetically tainted with "Russian fingerprints."

We do not think that the June 12, 14, & 15 timing was pure coincidence. Rather, it suggests the start of a pre-emptive move to associate Russia with anything WikiLeaks might have been about to publish and to "show" that it came from a Russian hack.

The Key Event

July 5, 2016: In the early evening, Eastern Daylight Time, someone working in the EDT time zone with a computer directly connected to the DNC server or DNC Local Area Network, copied 1,976 MegaBytes of data in 87 seconds onto an external storage device. **THAT SPEED IS MUCH FASTER THAN WHAT IS PHYSICALLY POSSIBLE WITH A HACK.**

It thus appears that the purported "hack" of the DNC by Guccifer 2.0 (the self-proclaimed WikiLeaks source) was not a hack by Russia or anyone else, but was rather a copy of DNC data onto an external storage device.

"Obfuscation & De-obfuscation"

Mr. President, the disclosure described below may be related. Even if it is not, it is something we think you should be made aware of in this general connection. On March 7, 2017, WikiLeaks began to publish a trove of original CIA documents that WikiLeaks labeled "Vault 7." WikiLeaks said it got the trove from a current or former CIA contractor and described it as comparable in scale and significance to the information Edward Snowden gave to reporters in 2013.

No one has challenged the authenticity of the original documents of Vault 7, which disclosed a vast array of cyber warfare tools developed, probably with help from NSA, by CIA's Engineering Development Group. That Group was part of the sprawling CIA Directorate of Digital Innovation – a growth industry established by John Brennan in 2015.

Scarcely imaginable digital tools – that can take control of your car and make it race over 100 mph, for example, or can enable remote spying through a TV – were described and duly reported in the New York Times and other media throughout March. But the Vault 7, part 3 release on March 31 that exposed the "Marble Framework" program apparently was judged too delicate to qualify as "news fit to print" and was kept out of the Times.

The Washington Post's Ellen Nakashima, it seems, "did not get the memo" in time. Her March 31 article bore the catching (and accurate) headline: **"WikiLeaks' latest release of CIA cyber-tools could blow the cover on agency hacking operations."**

The WikiLeaks release indicated that Marble was designed for flexible and easy-to-use "obfuscation," and that Marble source code includes a "deobfuscator" to reverse CIA text obfuscation.

More important, the CIA reportedly used Marble during 2016. In her Washington Post report, Nakashima left that out, but did include another significant point made by WikiLeaks; namely, that the obfuscation tool could be used to conduct a "forensic attribution double game" or false-flag operation because it included test samples in Chinese, Russian, Korean, Arabic and Farsi.

The CIA's reaction was neuralgic. Director Mike Pompeo lashed out two weeks later, calling Assange and his associates "demons," and insisting; "It's time to call out WikiLeaks for what it really is, a non-state hostile intelligence service, often abetted by state actors like Russia."

Mr. President, we do not know if CIA's Marble Framework, or tools like it, played some kind of role in the campaign to blame Russia for hacking the DNC. Nor do we know how candid the denizens of CIA's Digital Innovation Directorate have been with you and with Director Pompeo. These are areas that might profit from early White House review.

Putin and the Technology

We also do not know if you have discussed cyber issues in any detail with President Putin. In his interview with NBC's Megyn Kelly, he seemed quite willing – perhaps even eager – to address issues related to the kind of cyber tools revealed in the Vault 7 disclosures, if only to indicate he has been briefed on them. Putin pointed out that today's technology enables hacking to be "masked and camouflaged to an extent that no one can understand the origin" [of the hack] … And, vice versa, it is possible to set up any entity or any individual that everyone will think that they are the exact source of that attack."

"Hackers may be anywhere," he said. "There may be hackers, by the way, in the United States who very craftily and professionally passed the buck to Russia. Can't you imagine such a scenario? … I can."

Full Disclosure: Over recent decades the ethos of our intelligence profession has eroded in the public mind to the point that agenda-free analysis is deemed well nigh impossible. Thus, we add this disclaimer, which applies to everything we in VIPS say and do: We have no political agenda; our sole purpose is to spread truth around and, when necessary, hold to account our former intelligence colleagues. We speak and write without fear or favor. Consequently, any resemblance between what we say and what presidents, politicians and pundits say is purely coincidental. The fact we find it is necessary to include that reminder speaks volumes about these highly politicized times. This is our 50th VIPS Memorandum since the afternoon of Powell's speech at the UN.

Links to the 49 past memos are found at
https://consortiumnews.com/vips-memos/.

VETERAN INTELLIGENCE PROFESSIONALS FOR SANITY

William Binney, former NSA Technical Director for World Geopolitical & Military Analysis; Co-founder of NSA's Signals Intelligence Automation Research Center

Skip Folden, independent analyst, retired IBM Program Manager for Information Technology US (Associate VIPS)

Matthew Hoh, former Capt., USMC, Iraq & Foreign Service Officer, Afghanistan (associate VIPS)

Larry C Johnson, CIA & State Department (ret.)

Michael S. Kearns, Air Force Intelligence Officer (Ret.), Master SERE Resistance to Interrogation Instructor

John Kiriakou, Former CIA Counterterrorism Officer and former Senior Investigator, Senate Foreign Relations Committee

Linda Lewis, WMD preparedness policy analyst, USDA (ret.)

Lisa Ling, TSgt USAF (ret.) (associate VIPS)

Edward Loomis, Jr., former NSA Technical Director for the Office of Signals Processing

David MacMichael, National Intelligence Council (ret.)

Ray McGovern, former U.S. Army Infantry/Intelligence officer and CIA analyst

Elizabeth Murray, former Deputy National Intelligence Officer for Middle East, CIA

Coleen Rowley, FBI Special Agent and former Minneapolis Division Legal Counsel (ret.)

Cian Westmoreland, former USAF Radio Frequency Transmission Systems Technician and Unmanned Aircraft Systems whistleblower (Associate VIPS)

Kirk Wiebe, former Senior Analyst, SIGINT Automation Research Center, NSA

Sarah G. Wilton, Intelligence Officer, DIA (ret.); Commander, US Naval Reserve (ret.)

Ann Wright, U.S. Army Reserve Colonel (ret) and former U.S. Diplomat

G. Seth Rich, Wikileaks and the DNC

Seth Rich was manager of voting data at the DNC. He was murdered in July 2016, but the media won't report on this or any of the related deaths listed below. Are the deaths being investigated?

2016

4/18: John Jones, lawyer who defended Assange, run over by train.
May: Michael Ratner (Wikileaks NY lawyer), cancer.
6/22: John Ashe, UN official, found dead with a barbell on his neck.
6/23: Mike Flynn, 48, reported on Clinton Foundation (unknown).
7/10: Seth Rich, DNC staffer, shot twice in back.
7/25: Joe Montano, 47, DNC, heart attack day before DNC convention.
8/01: Victor Thorn, gunshot wound, author of books on Clintons.
8/02: Shawn Lucas, DNC process server, combination of drugs.
Oct: Gavin McFayden (Wikileaks founder), cancer.
Nov: Monica Petersen, Clinton Foundation investigator found dead

2017

May: Peter Smith, GOP operative, found dead from asphyxiation in a Minnesota hotel room just days after talking to the Wall Street Journal about his efforts to obtain Hillary's Clinton's missing emails.
May: Beranton Whisenant, a prosecutor investigating the DNC, was found dead on a Hollywood, FL beach.
July: Klaus Eberwein, former Haiti Government official, found dead in a motel room with a gunshot wound to the head. He was about to testify on Clinton Foundation connection to the Haitian earthquake.
July: Joseph Rago was a 34 year old, WSJ reporter. He was researching for info on Clinton and was found dead. Cause of death unknown.
Aug: Kurt Smolek had possible ties to PizzaGate and child trafficking in Cambodia, found dead in the Potomac River. Up until 2015, Smolek worked for the State Dept in Cambodia as an OSAC Diplomatic Security Agent.

What is the probability that in a random group of N individuals, n would die unnaturally in T years, given the group weighted average mortality rate R? The expected number of unnatural deaths is E = N*R*T. The **Poisson distribution function** calculates the probability of rare events. The probability of n homicides when E are expected is P = poisson (n, E, false).

Assume N = 10,000 DNC/Wikileaks related individuals:
– 8 suspicious deaths (5 homicides) in 3 months from April 2016.
The probability is 1 in 6.5 million.

– 15 suspicious deaths (11 homicides) in 16 months since April 2016.
T= 1.3 years (68 weeks), the probability P = 1 in 7.8 billion.
If N = 30,000: The probability of 11 homicides is 1 in 145,000.

If the 11 unnatural deaths were a combination of 8 homicides, 1 accident and 2 suicides, the weighted average mortality rate is 0.00009. The probability P= 1 in 14.5 million. But the "accidents" and "suicides" were likely homicides

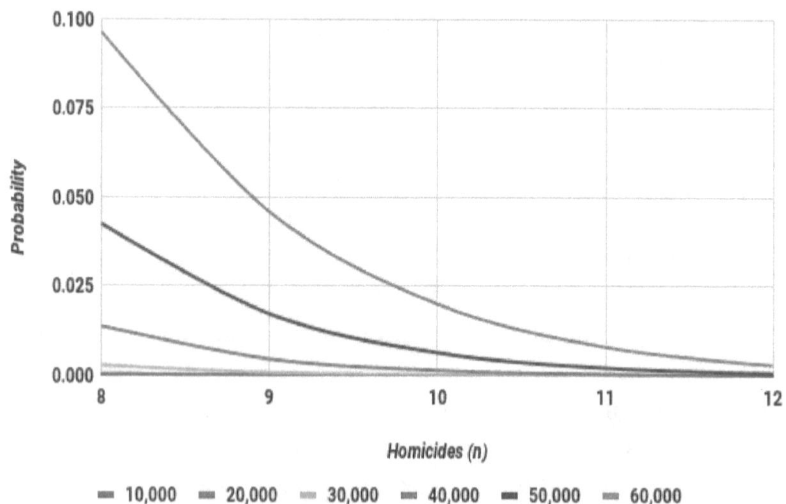

H. Track Record: 1988-2016

1988-2008 State and National Presidential True Vote Model
https://docs.google.com/spreadsheet/ccc?key=0AjAk1JUWDMyRd
GN3WEZNTUFaR0tfOHVXTzA1VGRsdHc#gid=0

1968-2012 National Presidential True Vote Model
https://docs.google.com/spreadsheet/ccc?key=0AjAk1JUWDMyRd
FpDLXZmWUFFLUFQSTVjWXM2ZGtsV0E#gid=4

1988 (24 unadjusted state exit polls)
Recorded Vote: Bush 53.4-Dukakis 45.7%
True Vote Model: Dukakis 50.2-48.8%
Unadjusted National Exit Poll: Dukakis 49.8-49.1%
Unadjusted State Exit Polls aggregate: Dukakis 51.6-47.3%
https://docs.google.com/spreadsheet/ccc?key=0AjAk1JUWDMyRd
FIzSTJtMTJZekNBWUdtbWp3bHlpWGc#gid=13

1992
Recorded Vote: Clinton 43.0-Bush 37.4%
True Vote Model: Clinton: 51.1-30.4%
Unadjusted National Exit Poll: Clinton: 46.3-33.5%
Unadjusted State Exit Polls aggregate: Clinton: 47.6-31.7%
https://docs.google.com/spreadsheet/ccc?key=0AjAk1JUWDMyRd
FIzSTJtMTJZekNBWUdtbWp3bHlpWGc#gid=17

1996
Recorded Vote: Clinton 49.2-Dole 40.8%
True Vote Model: Clinton 53.6-36.5%
Unadjusted National Exit Poll: Clinton 52.2-37.5%
Unadjusted State Exit Polls aggregate: Clinton 52.7-37.0%
https://docs.google.com/spreadsheet/ccc?key=0AjAk1JUWDMyRd
FIzSTJtMTJZekNBWUdtbWp3bHlpWGc#gid=16

2000

Recorded Vote: Gore 48.4-Bush 47.9%

True Vote Model: Gore 51.5-44.7%

Unadjusted National Exit Poll: Gore 48.5-46.3%

Unadjusted State Exit Polls aggregate: Gore 50.8-44.4%

https://richardcharnin.wordpress.com/2011/11/21/unadjusted-state-exit-polls-indicate-that-al-gore-won-a-mini-landslide-in-2000/
https://docs.google.com/spreadsheet/ccc?key=0AjAk1JUWDMyRd FIzSTJtMTJZekNBWUdtbWp3bHlpWGc#gid=4

2004

Recorded Vote: Bush 50.7-Kerry 48.3%, 255 EV

Election Forecast Model: Kerry 51.8%, 337 EV (snapshot)

True Vote Model: Kerry 53.6-45.1%, 364 EV

Unadjusted National Exit Poll: Kerry 51.7-47.0%

Unadjusted State Exit Polls aggregate: Kerry 51.1-47.6%, 337 EV

https://richardcharnin.wordpress.com/2012/02/21/the-final-2004-national-exit-poll-switched-7-2-of-kerry-responders-to-bush/
https://docs.google.com/spreadsheet/ccc?key=0AjAk1JUWDMyRd GN3WEZNTUFaR0tfOHVXTzA1VGRsdHc#gid=0

2008

Recorded Vote: Obama 52.9-McCain 45.6%, 365 EV

Election Forecast Model: Obama 53.1%, 365.3 EV (simulation mean)

True Vote Model: Obama 58.0-40.4%, 420 EV

Unadjusted National Exit Poll: Obama 61.0-37.2%

Unadjusted State Exit Polls aggregate: Obama 58.0-40.5%, 420 EV

http://www.richardcharnin.com/2008ElectionModel.htm
https://docs.google.com/spreadsheet/ccc?key=0AjAk1JUWDMyRd FIzSTJtMTJZekNBWUdtbWp3bHlpWGc#gid=1

2012

Recorded vote: Obama 51.0-Romney 47.2%, 332 EV
Election Forecast (2-party): Obama 51.6-Romney 48.4%, 332 EV
True Vote Model: Obama 55.2%, 380 EV

https://richardcharnin.wordpress.com/2012/11/05/final-forecast-the-2012-true-vote-election-fraud-model/
Unadjusted National Exit Poll unavailable
Unadjusted State Exit polls unavailable (19 states not polled)

2016

Recorded Vote: Clinton 48.3-46.2%, Trump 306-232 EV
Recorded Vote Forecast: Trump 44.4-42.9% with 306-232 EV
True Vote Model: Trump 48.5-44.3% with 351-187 EV
Unadjusted National Exit Poll unavailable
Unadjusted 28 State Exit polls: Clinton 47.9-44.7%

https://richardcharnin.wordpress.com/2016/11/07/2016-election-model-forecast/
https://docs.google.com/spreadsheets/d/1sGxtIofohrj3POpwq-85Id2_fYKgvgoWbPZacZw0XlY/edit#gid=1739803045

I. Reference Links

2016 Presidential Election Model
https://docs.google.com/spreadsheets/d/1R9Y3ae2uyW8SUxVUnn
Ot9ZyvheAxa0fAhesAw_nhciM/edit#gid=0

2016 Presidential State Election Model
https://docs.google.com/spreadsheets/d/10dlTnin814phKJWjYdkG-
ujNKak3zo6ywIP0u0-TGFg/edit#gid=1036175945

Gallup News, "Party Affiliation",
http://www.gallup.com/poll/15370/party-affiliation.aspx

Gallup News, "Democratic, Republican Identification near
Historical Lows", http://news.gallup.com/poll/188096/democratic-
republican-identification-near-historical-lows.aspx

TDMS Research
http://tdmsresearch.com/wp-content/uploads/2016/11/2016-
Presidential-Election-Table_Nov-17.-2016.jpg
http://tdmsresearch.com/2016/11/10/2016-presidential-election-
table/

Bev Harris, "Fraction Magic- Part 1: Votes are being counted as
fractions instead of as whole numbers:"
http://blackboxvoting.org/fraction-magic-1/

Dawn Pappel, "Election Justice USA on California Primary: Early
Voter Poll Yields 23% Discrepancy with Vote-by-Mail totals",
Inquisitor
http://www.inquisitr.com/3202381/election-justice-on-california-
primary-early-voter-exit-poll-yields-23-discrepancy-with-l-a-vote-
by-mail-totals/#y2htCZ1YrCQapYPK.99

Roger Stone, *Can the 2016 election be rigged? You bet*, The Hill

"Noncitizens, Voting Violations and U.S. Elections", FAIR
https://fairus.org/issue/societal-impact/noncitizens-voting-
violations-and-us-elections

Kim Zetter, "Unique Transparency Program Uncovers Problems
with Voting Software", WIRED
https://www.wired.com/2008/12/unique-transpar/

Greg Palast, "The Election Was Stolen – Here's How…"
http://www.gregpalast.com/election-stolen-heres/

Jim Hoft, "10 of 11 California Counties with More Registered
Voters than Voting Age Adults Are Democrat",
Gateway Pundit
http://www.thegatewaypundit.com/2017/08/10-11-california-
counties-registered-voters-voting-age-adults-democrat/

Rick Moran, "Report: As Many as 5.7 Million Non-Citizens Voted
in the 2008 election", PJ Media
https://pjmedia.com/trending/2017/06/20/report-as-many-as-5-7-
million-non-citizens-voted-in-2008-election

Joe Kovacs, "Obama Encourages Illegals to Vote", WMD
http://www.wnd.com/2016/11/obama-encourages-illegal-aliens-to-
vote/

Joshua Philipp, "Voting Machines in 16 States Tied to George
Soros Ally" http://www.theepochtimes.com/n3/2176907-voting-
machines-in-16-states-tied-to-george-soros-ally/

Daavid Krayden, "Soros-Connected Company Has Provided Voting
Technology in 16 States"
http://dailycaller.com/2016/10/18/soros-connected-company-
provides-voting-machines-in-16-states/

Joel Kurth and Jonathan Oosting, "Records: Too many votes in
37% of Detroit's precincts", Detroit News
http://www.detroitnews.com/story/news/politics/2016/12/12/records
-many-votes-detroits-precincts/95363314/

Deroy Murdock, "America might have 3.5 million more voters than eligible adult citizens", Dallas News
https://www.dallasnews.com/opinion/commentary/2017/08/11/america-may-35-million-voters-eligible-adult-citizens

Ray Lutz, "Bernie vs. Hillary Recount in San Diego", Citizens Oversight
http://www.copswiki.org/Common/SanDiegoPrimaryRecount2016

Project Censored, "Clintonistas/DNC Illegally Stole the Democratic Primaries from Bernie Sanders"
http://projectcensored.org/clintonistasdnc-illegally-stole-democratic-primaries-bernie-sanders/

Amy Chozick
"Hillary Clinton Targets Republicans Turned Off by Donald Trump", NY Times
https://www.nytimes.com/2016/05/07/us/politics/hillary-clinton-republican-party.html

MJ Lee, "Donald Trump's new target: Bernie Sanders supporters"
http://www.cnn.com/2016/04/29/politics/donald-trump-bernie-sanders/

Jeffery Kutler "Technology Raises Election Fraud Issues But May Hold Solutions Too", Institutional Investor
https://www.institutionalinvestor.com/article/b150zrw4p2284m/technology-raises-election-fraud-issues-but-may-hold-solutions-too

Book Reviews

Reclaiming Science: The JFK Conspiracy

Judyth Vary Baker
Author of 'Me and Lee' and 'David Ferrie'
Richard Charnin is a mathematician whose abilities are well used to present for us the chilling reality: it's not been safe to be an easily-found witness who might say the wrong thing about the Kennedy assassination. Can serve as a handbook for anyone who wants to teach the next generation about the outright lies and obfuscations by the Warren Commission

Robert Kirkconnell
Author of 'American Heart of Darkness'
Finally, the math and science that has been meticulously avoided by the Pathocracy! Richard has hit one out of the park with statistical analysis of what happened and the probability that what the US government said happened was impossible.

Philip A. Stahl
Author of 'The JFK Assassination- The Final Analysis',
'Reclaiming Science: The JFK Conspiracy' features an apt title because it entails reclaiming the legitimate content that has hitherto been obfuscated and distorted under the specious science (or what I call pseudo-science) of the Warren Commission Report as well as the apologists like Gerald Posner ('Case Closed') and Vince Bugliosi ('Reclaiming History'). Charnin's book is the perfect antidote to the specious science circulated by a complicit media (Google 'Operation Mockingbird' for more information)

Midwest Book Review
Charnin works as a mathematician right out of the belly of the beast, having served as a "numerical control programmer" in the defense industry and for corporate Wall Street investment banks. The book resolves the history of a debate about the real probabilities concerning the witness death list, long seen as unusual by simple common sense observation. Reclaiming Science presents a footnote to a long debate where, in the end, the available math data finally caught up with the common sense observation.

Matrix of Deceit: Forcing Pre-election and Exit Polls to Match Fraudulent Vote Counts

Michael Carmichael
Explodes the Myth of American Democracy
Richard Charnin, a formidable quant with an amazing gift for Monte Carlo Simulations and the world's most sophisticated mathematical analysis of election fraud, has written an important book for the general public.

David Wayne
co-author with Richard Belzer of 'Dead Wrong' and 'Hit List'
There couldn't be more important work at a more important time than this analysis of our voting process. There is no process more integral and vital to our democracy -- and the integrity of the process should not be negotiable. Richard Charnin's simple math PROVES that our electoral process requires immediate attention.